"Master Life"

growth. wisdom. balance.

MASTERING TOKENOMICS

The Ultimate Guide

by

DENNIS FRANK

Copyright Notice

Cover design by -
KRYPTOKRAKEN™ Productions

Portions of this book were created and/or edited with the assistance of an AI Co-pilot.

First Print Edition, January 2024

This book was originally published in electronic format in January 2024.

Produced in the United States of America

KRYPTOKRAKEN™ PRODUCTIONS

DEDICATION

This book is dedicated to Eva, my wife, for all her love, understanding, and patience as I spent innumerable hours putting this document together.

"In the ever-evolving landscape of cryptocurrency, preparation is key; it's like planting seeds today for a garden of opportunity tomorrow." - Dennis Frank

TABLE OF CONTENTS

COPYRIGHT NOTICE IV

DEDICATION VI

1.1: UNDERSTANDING THE CONTEXT OF TOKENOMICS 1

1.2: THE EVOLUTION OF DIGITAL TOKENS...........................4

1.3: KEY COMPONENTS OF TOKENOMICS 7

1.4: THE INSTITUTIONALIZED SYSTEMS IN TOKENOMICS 9

1.5: THE ROLE OF TOKENOMICS IN FACILITATING TRANSACTIONS 11

1.6: THE FUNCTIONALITY OF TOKENS IN THEIR RESPECTIVE ECOSYSTEMS 13

1.7: THE INTERPLAY BETWEEN TOKENOMICS AND TRADITIONAL ECONOMICS 16

1.8: INTRODUCTION TO TOKEN VALUATION 19

1.9: THE FUTURE OF TOKENOMICS 22

2.1: UNDERSTANDING DIGITAL TOKENS 25

2.2: UTILITY TOKENS 28

2.3: SECURITY TOKENS 31

2.4: GOVERNANCE TOKENS 33

2.5: NON-FUNGIBLE TOKENS (NFTS) 35

2.6: OTHER TYPES OF TOKENS 37

2.7: TOKEN STANDARDS 39

2.8: TOKEN USE CASES ACROSS INDUSTRIES 41

2.9: THE ROLE OF TOKENS IN DECENTRALIZED FINANCE (DEFI) 44

3.1: INTRODUCTION TO TOKEN CREATION AND DISTRIBUTION MECHANISMS 47

3.2: INITIAL COIN OFFERINGS (ICOS) 50

3.3: SECURITY TOKEN OFFERINGS (STOS) 53

3.4: AIRDROPS AS A DISTRIBUTION MECHANISM 56

3.5: FORKS IN TOKEN CREATION AND DISTRIBUTION 59

3.6: OTHER DISTRIBUTION STRATEGIES.................................61

3.7: LEGAL AND REGULATORY CONSIDERATIONS IN TOKEN CREATION 64

3.8: BEST PRACTICES AND PITFALLS   IN TOKEN CREATION AND DISTRIBUTION 67

3.9: THE FUTURE OF TOKEN CREATION AND DISTRIBUTION 71

4.1: UNDERSTANDING ECONOMIC MODELS IN TOKENOMICS 74

4.2: INCENTIVE STRUCTURES IN TOKEN-BASED SYSTEMS 77

4.3: UNDERSTANDING TOKEN VELOCITY 80

4.4: TOKEN BURN MECHANISMS AND DEFLATIONARY MODELS.................83

4.5: NETWORK EFFECTS IN TOKENOMICS 85

4.6: CASE STUDIES OF ECONOMIC MODELS IN TOKENOMICS.......................88

4.7: EMERGING TRENDS IN ECONOMIC MODELS IN TOKENOMICS 91

4.8: REVIEW AND FUTURE OUTLOOK OF ECONOMIC MODELS IN TOKENOMICS 94

5.1: NAVIGATING GLOBAL REGULATORY FRAMEWORKS 97

5.2: LEGAL CHALLENGES IN TOKEN ISSUANCE AND MANAGEMENT............100

5.3: ANTI-MONEY LAUNDERING AND KNOW YOUR CUSTOMER COMPLIANCE 103

5.4: CASE STUDIES OF REGULATORY IMPACT ON TOKENOMICS 106

6.1: UNDERSTANDING CASE STUDIES IN TOKENOMICS................108

6.2: SUCCESS STORIES IN TOKENOMICS 111

6.3: LESSONS FROM FAILED TOKEN PROJECTS 114

6.4: CASE STUDY: BITCOIN AND ITS IMPACT ON TOKENOMICS 116

6.5: CASE STUDY: ETHEREUM AND THE RISE OF SMART CONTRACTS 118

6.6: CASE STUDY: DEFI TOKENS AND YIELD FARMING.................120

6.7: CASE STUDY: NFTS AND THE TOKENIZATION OF DIGITAL ASSETS..........122

TOKENOMICS FROM PAST CASE STUDIES 124

6.9: REVIEW AND ANALYSIS OF REAL-WORLD APPLICATIONS....................127

6.10: CASE STUDY ANALYSIS AND DISCUSSION 130

7.1: UNDERSTANDING MARKET SENTIMENT IN TOKENOMICS 133

7.2: FACTORS INFLUENCING TOKEN PRICING....................................136

7.3: INTRODUCTION TO TOKEN VALUATION MODELS................................139

7.4: IN-DEPTH ANALYSIS OF TOKEN VALUATION MODELS 142

7.5: TOKEN VALUATION FOR UTILITY TOKENS 145

7.6: TOKEN VALUATION FOR SECURITY TOKENS....................................148

7.7: TOKEN VALUATION FOR GOVERNANCE TOKENS AND NFTS 151

7.8: FUTURE TRENDS IN TOKEN VALUATION................................154

7.9: REVIEW AND ANALYSIS OF MARKET DYNAMICS AND TOKEN VALUATION 157

8.1: UNDERSTANDING THE UTILITY OF TOKENS 160

8.2: TOKENS IN GOVERNANCE AND DECISION MAKING...............................162

8.3: TOKENS IN DECENTRALIZED FINANCE (DEFI) APPLICATIONS 165

8.4: NON-FUNGIBLE TOKENS (NFTS) AND THEIR FUNCTIONALITY 168

8.5: TOKEN FUNCTIONALITY AND INTEROPERABILITY...............................171

8.6: TOKEN UTILITY AND FUNCTIONALITY: RISKS AND CHALLENGES............174

8.7: THE FUTURE OF TOKEN UTILITY AND FUNCTIONALITY 177

9.1: THE ROLE OF TOKENOMICS IN DEFI AND YIELD FARMING....................180

9.2: THE RISE OF DAOS AND COMMUNITY GOVERNANCE IN TOKENOMICS .183

9.3: INTERSECTION OF TOKENOMICS AND TRADITIONAL FINANCE.............186

9.4: THE IMPACT OF REGULATION ON THE FUTURE OF TOKENOMICS 189

9.5: THE ROLE OF TOKENOMICS IN THE FUTURE BLOCKCHAIN TECHNOLOGY 192

9.6: THE FUTURE OF TOKEN CREATION AND DISTRIBUTION MECHANISMS .195

9.7: THE FUTURE OF TOKEN VALUATION 198

9.8: THE FUTURE OF TOKEN UTILITY AND FUNCTIONALITY 201

9.9: EMERGING TRENDS AND FUTURE OF TOKENOMICS: A RECAP 204

GLOSSARY OF TOKENOMICS TERMS..207

MEET THE COURSE CREATOR 228

Welcome to "Mastering Tokenomics: The Ultimate Guide where blockchain innovation meets economic principles

This course simplifies the complexities of tokenomics, which is essential for navigating the digital asset landscape.

We'll explore everything from supply and demand in digital currencies to the mechanisms that drive token utility and value whether you're a digital finance expert or new to cryptocurrencies, this guide offers insights for all skill levels.

By mastering tokenomics, you'll learn to not only understand but also actively engage in the evolving world of digital finance.

Join me on this enlightening journey to harness the potential of digital currencies. Let's start exploring!

1.1: Understanding the Context of Tokenomics

Lesson Overview

In this lesson, we will introduce the concept of Tokenomics, its importance in the blockchain ecosystem, and its relationship with cryptocurrencies. By the end of this lesson, you will have a solid understanding of what Tokenomics is and why it's a crucial aspect of the digital currency world.

Definition of Tokenomics

Tokenomics, a portmanteau of 'token' and 'economics', is a study that focuses on the system of rules governing the distribution, usage, and value of digital tokens within a blockchain ecosystem.

It is the framework that defines how tokens work and how they are integrated into their respective systems. Tokenomics is not just about the token itself but also about the overall token environment, including the policies for token creation, management, and distribution.

The Importance of Tokenomics in the Blockchain Ecosystem

Tokenomics plays a vital role in the blockchain ecosystem. Here's why:

- **Incentivization:** Tokens can be used as incentives for network participants. For instance, miners in the Bitcoin network are rewarded with BTC tokens for validating transactions.

- **Value Transfer:** Tokens facilitate the transfer of value within the network. They can represent a wide range of digital or physical assets and can be exchanged for goods or services.

- **Governance:** Some tokens allow holders to participate in decentralized organizations' decision-making processes, influencing the project's direction.

Fundraising: Tokens are often used in Initial Coin Offerings (ICOs) and Security Token Offerings STOs) as a means of raising funds for blockchain projects funds for blockchain projects.

The Relationship Between Tokenomics and Cryptocurrencies

Tokenomics is integral to the functioning of cryptocurrencies. The value of a cryptocurrency is not just about its price in the market. It's also about its utility, demand, and the economic model that governs its supply.

Understanding Tokenomics can help investors make informed decisions. For instance, if a token's supply is unlimited, it might lead to inflation and decrease in value over time. On the other hand, a token with a deflationary model, where the supply decreases over time, might increase in value.

Tokenomics also helps in understanding the functionality of a token within its ecosystem. For example, Ether (ETH) is used to pay for transaction fees and computational services on the Ethereum network.

In the next lesson, we will delve deeper into the evolution of digital tokens and explore how they have transformed the digital economy

"Tokenomics: Where the digital pulse of innovation harmonizes with the rhythm of economic principles, creating a symphony of decentralized value."
- Dennis Frank

1.2: The Evolution of Digital Tokens

In this lesson, we will delve into the evolution of digital tokens, a journey that begins with the birth of Bitcoin and extends to the diverse landscape of altcoins and various token distribution methods we see today.

The Birth of Bitcoin and the First Digital Token

The history of digital tokens is inextricably linked to the birth of Bitcoin, the world's first cryptocurrency. In 2008, an anonymous entity known as Satoshi Nakamoto published the Bitcoin whitepaper, titled "Bitcoin: A Peer-to-Peer Electronic Cash System."

This revolutionary document laid the groundwork for the creation of the Bitcoin network, which went live in January 2009.

Bitcoin introduced the concept of digital tokens, which are essentially units of value within a blockchain network. In the case of Bitcoin, the digital token is the Bitcoin (BTC) itself. These tokens are not physical but exist as data on the blockchain, a decentralized ledger that records all transactions involving the tokens.

The Emergence of Altcoins and Token Diversity

While Bitcoin was the first, it certainly wasn't the last. The success of Bitcoin sparked a wave of innovation, leading to the creation of numerous other cryptocurrencies, collectively known as altcoins (alternative coins).

These altcoins, such as Ethereum, Ripple (XRP), and Litecoin, introduced their own unique digital tokens, expanding the diversity of the token ecosystem.

Ethereum, in particular, played a significant role in the evolution of digital tokens. Launched in 2015, Ethereum introduced the concept of smart contracts, self-executing contracts with the terms of the agreement directly written into code.

This innovation allowed for the creation of Ethereum's token standard, ERC-20, which made it easy for anyone to create their own digital tokens on the Ethereum blockchain. This led to an explosion of new digital tokens, each with its own unique functionalities and use cases.

The Evolution and Impact of ICOs, STOs, and Other Token Distribution Methods

The introduction of ERC-20 and similar token standards on other blockchains facilitated the rise of new token distribution methods. The most notable of these is the Initial Coin Offering (ICO), a crowdfunding method where a company or project sells its own digital tokens to raise funds.

ICOs became incredibly popular during the 2017 cryptocurrency boom, leading to a wild west of sorts in the token world. However, the lack of regulation also led to many fraudulent ICOs, prompting a crackdown by regulatory bodies worldwide.

In response to the regulatory challenges of ICOs, the concept of Security Token Offerings (STOs) emerged. STOs are like ICOs but are designed to fall within securities regulations, providing a safer and more legally compliant method of token distribution. Other token distribution methods, such as airdrops (free distribution of tokens), forks (splitting a blockchain into two, creating new tokens), and Initial Exchange Offerings (IEOs), have also evolved over time, each with its own unique advantages and challenges.

The evolution of digital tokens has been a journey of innovation, diversity, and regulatory challenges. From the birth of Bitcoin to the diverse landscape of tokens we see today, digital tokens have fundamentally reshaped the world of finance and beyond.

As we move forward, it's clear that digital tokens will continue to evolve, offering new possibilities and challenges alike.

In the next lesson, we will explore the key components of Tokenomics, providing a deeper understanding of the systems and mechanisms that underpin the functionality of digital tokens.

"From ICOs to STOs and beyond, the evolution of token distribution mirrors a journey of innovation and adaptation, navigating through the dynamic seas of regulation and opportunity in the digital finance world." - Dennis Frank

1.3: Key Components of Tokenomics

In this lesson, we will delve into the key components of Tokenomics. Understanding these elements is crucial to comprehending the overall dynamics of the token economy. We will focus on three main points: the role of supply and demand, token velocity, and the importance of utility in token value.

The Role of Supply and Demand in Tokenomics

Just like in traditional economics, supply and demand play a pivotal role in Tokenomics. The value of a token often depends on its supply (how many tokens are available) and demand (how many people want to buy these tokens).

- **Supply:** In the context of Tokenomics, the supply of a token can be either fixed or dynamic. For example, Bitcoin has a fixed supply of 21 million coins, which means no more will ever be created. On the other hand, some tokens have a dynamic supply that can increase, or decrease based on certain conditions.

- **Demand:** The demand for a token depends on several factors such as its utility (what you can with the token), the popularity of the project, the size of the user base, and market sentiment. High demand coupled with limited supply often leads to an increase in token price.

Understanding Token Velocity

Token velocity refers to how often a token is exchanged or used. It is a critical component of Tokenomics as it impacts the token's value. High token velocity means that tokens are frequently traded or used, which can lead to a decrease in token value if the supply is high. Conversely, low token velocity, where tokens are held for longer periods, can lead to an increase in token value, especially if the supply is limited.

Understanding token velocity can help in designing the token's economic model, including its distribution and incentive mechanisms.

The Importance of Utility in Token Value

Utility refers to the usefulness or functionality of a token within its ecosystem. The utility of a token is a key determinant of its value. Tokens with high utility have more demand as they can be used for various purposes within their ecosystem.

For example, Ether (ETH), the native token of the Ethereum blockchain, is used to pay for transaction fees, deploy smart contracts, and participate in decentralized applications (dApps) built on Ethereum. This high utility drives demand for ETH, contributing to its value.

In contrast, tokens with low or no utility may see less demand, leading to lower value. Therefore, when designing a token, it is crucial to ensure it has a defined utility that adds value to its ecosystem.

In conclusion, understanding the role of supply and demand, token velocity, and utility in token value is crucial in mastering Tokenomics. These components form the backbone of the token economy and influence the functionality and value of tokens in their respective ecosystems. In the next lesson, we will explore the institutionalized systems in Tokenomics.

> "The stock market is filled with individuals who know the price of everything, but the value of nothing." - Philip Fisher

1.4: The Institutionalized Systems in Tokenomics

The Role of Blockchain in Tokenomics

Blockchain technology plays a pivotal role in the field of Tokenomics. The underlying technology enables the creation, distribution, and transaction of digital tokens.

The blockchain is a decentralized, distributed ledger that records every transaction of a digital token, ensuring transparency and security. The blockchain's decentralized nature eliminates the need for a central authority or intermediary, such as a bank or a government, to validate transactions.

This decentralization is a fundamental principle of Tokenomics, as it allows for democratizing financial systems and creating a truly global economy.

Blockchain technology also provides the infrastructure for creating and implementing smart contracts, which are crucial for facilitating transactions in Tokenomics.

Smart Contracts and Transaction Facilitation

Smart contracts are self-executing contracts with the terms of the agreement directly written into code. They automatically execute transactions when certain predefined conditions are met.

In the context of Tokenomics, smart contracts play a crucial role in facilitating transactions, such as the transfer of digital tokens from one party to another.

Smart contracts bring efficiency, transparency, and trust to the transaction process. They reduce the risk of fraud, as the contract execution is automated and does not rely on a single party. Moreover, smart contracts can be programmed to implement complex logic and business rules, enabling the creation of sophisticated token economies.

The Importance of Decentralization in Tokenomics

Decentralization is a key principle of Tokenomics. It refers to the distribution of authority, decision-making, and control across a network, rather than being concentrated in a single central authority.

In a decentralized system, anyone can participate, contribute, and make decisions depending on the rules set by the token economy. Decentralization brings numerous benefits to Tokenomics. It increases security, as there is no central point of failure that can be attacked. It enhances privacy, as transactions are not controlled by a single entity that can monitor and censor them. It promotes fairness and inclusivity, as everyone can participate in the token economy.

Moreover, decentralization enables the creation of decentralized autonomous organizations (DAOs), where token holders conduct governance and decision-making. This leads to more democratic and transparent systems, fostering trust and cooperation among participants.

In conclusion, the institutionalized systems in Tokenomics, including blockchain technology, smart contracts, and decentralization, are fundamental to the creation, operation, and success of token economies. They provide the necessary infrastructure, facilitate transactions, and uphold the principles of transparency, security, and inclusivity.

1.5: The Role of Tokenomics in Facilitating Transactions

In this lesson, we will delve into the role of Tokenomics in facilitating transactions within the blockchain ecosystem. We will discuss how tokens are used as a medium of exchange, the role of tokens in incentivizing network participation, and the impact of Tokenomics on transaction costs and efficiency.

Tokens as a Medium of Exchange

One of the fundamental roles of tokens in the blockchain ecosystem is to serve as a medium of exchange. Tokens can be transferred between parties in a transaction, making them an integral part of the blockchain's economic system. This is akin to how money is used in traditional economies.

For instance, in the Ethereum blockchain, Ether (ETH) is used as a medium to facilitate transactions and pay for computational services. Similarly, in the Bitcoin network, Bitcoin (BTC) is used to reward miners for adding new transactions to the blockchain.

Incentivizing Network Participation

Tokens also play a crucial role in incentivizing network participation. In many blockchain networks, tokens are used as rewards for network participants who contribute to the network's maintenance and security. This incentive mechanism encourages more users to participate in the network, thereby enhancing the network's overall security and functionality.

For example, in Proof-of-Work (PoW) systems like Bitcoin, miners are rewarded with BTC for solving complex mathematical problems to add new blocks to the blockchain. In Proof-of-Stake (PoS) systems like Ethereum 2.0, validators are rewarded with ETH for proposing and attesting to new blocks.

11

Impact on Transaction Costs and Efficiency

Tokenomics also has a significant impact on transaction costs and efficiency. In traditional financial systems, transaction costs are often high due to the involvement of intermediaries. However, in blockchain networks, transactions are peer-to-peer, which significantly reduces costs.

Moreover, the use of tokens in transactions also enhances efficiency. Transactions can be completed in real time, regardless of the geographical location of the parties involved. This is a stark contrast to traditional financial systems, where cross-border transactions can take several days to complete.

In conclusion, Tokenomics plays a pivotal role in facilitating transactions in the blockchain ecosystem. By serving as a medium of exchange, incentivizing network participation, and enhancing transaction efficiency, tokens are at the heart of blockchain's revolutionary potential.

In the next lesson, we will explore the functionality of tokens in their respective ecosystems.

1.6: The Functionality of Tokens in Their Respective Ecosystems

Digital tokens, the heart of any blockchain ecosystem, serve multiple functions depending on their design and purpose. Let's delve into the three primary types of tokens:

1. **Utility Tokens:** These tokens provide users with access to a product or service within a specific blockchain ecosystem. For instance, Filecoin (FIL) is a utility token that allows users to access decentralized storage services.

2. **Security Tokens:** These tokens represent an investment contract into an underlying investment asset, such as stocks, bonds, funds, and real estate. They derive their value from an external, tradable asset and are subject to federal securities regulations.

3. **Governance Tokens:** These tokens allow holders to vote on decisions that affect the blockchain network, thereby giving them a say in the project's direction. An example is Uniswap's UNI token, which enables holders to vote on proposals related to the platform's development.

How Tokens Contribute to the Health and Growth of Their Ecosystems

Tokens play a crucial role in the growth and sustainability of their respective ecosystems, Here's how:

1. **Incentivization:** Tokens incentivize network participants to contribute to the ecosystem, whether by validating transactions, providing liquidity, or participating in governance.

2. **Value Exchange:** Tokens facilitate the exchange of value within the ecosystem, acting as a medium of exchange for goods and services.

3. **Fundraising:** Tokens, particularly those issued through Initial Coin Offerings (ICOs) or Security Token Offerings (STOs), help projects raise funds for development and expansion.

The Role of Tokens in Network Security and Consensus Mechanisms

Tokens also play a pivotal role in maintaining network security and facilitating consensus mechanisms in blockchain ecosystems.

1. **Proof-of-Stake (PoS) and its Variants:** In PoS-based blockchains, token holders can 'stake' their tokens to become validators and earn rewards for validating transactions. This mechanism enhances network security as malicious actors would need to control a significant portion of the token supply to attack the network, which is economically unfeasible.

2. **Delegated Proof-of-Stake (DPoS):** In DPoS blockchains, token holders can vote for delegates to validate transactions on their behalf. The delegates are incentivized to act honestly as dishonest behavior could lead to them losing their delegate status.

3. **Proof-of-Authority (PoA):** In PoA blockchains, a set number of 'authorities' are given the right to validate transactions. These authorities are often chosen based on the number of tokens they hold, their reputation, or their contribution to the ecosystem.

In conclusion, tokens are not just digital assets; they are the life-blood of blockchain ecosystems, driving growth, facilitating value exchange, maintaining network security, and enabling de-centralized governance. Understanding their functionality is crucial to mastering the concept of Tokenomics.

"Change is the only constant in life. One's ability to adapt to those changes will determine your success in life." - Benjamin Franklin

1.7: The Interplay Between Tokenomics And Traditional Economics

Introduction

In this lesson, we will explore the interplay between Tokenomics and traditional economics. We will delve into the comparison between traditional economic models and Tokenomics, understand how Tokenomics challenges traditional financial systems, and discuss the potential of Tokenomics to disrupt traditional economic structures.

Comparison between Traditional Economic Models and Tokenomics

Traditional economic models are based on the principles of supply and demand, production and consumption, and the role of money as a medium of exchange. These models often assume that all actors are rational and that markets are efficient.

On the other hand, Tokenomics introduces a new paradigm where tokens, which are digital assets with inherent value, play a central role. Tokens can represent a wide range of assets and rights, from ownership and voting rights to access to services.

This flexibility allows for the creation of innovative economic models that can be customized to the specific needs of a blockchain ecosystem.

How Tokenomics Challenges Traditional Financial Systems

Tokenomics challenges traditional financial systems in several ways. First, it introduces a new form of value exchange that does not rely on central authorities or intermediaries. This decentralization can reduce costs and increase efficiency, but it also raises new regulatory and security challenges.

Second, Tokenomics enables the creation of programmable money. Tokens can be programmed with specific rules and conditions, enabling the automation of complex financial transactions and contracts. This programmability can disrupt traditional financial services, from banking and payments to insurance and asset management.

Finally, Tokenomics allows for the tokenization of any asset, from physical goods to intellectual property. This tokenization can democratize access to assets and investment opportunities, but it also requires new valuation models and risk management strategies.

The Potential of Tokenomics to Disrupt Traditional Economic Structures

Tokenomics has the potential to disrupt traditional economic structures in profound ways. Tokenomics can create more inclusive, efficient, and innovative economic systems by enabling peer-to-peer value exchange, programmable money, and asset tokenization.

However, this potential also comes with significant challenges. The regulatory landscape for tokens is still evolving, and there are significant risks related to security, privacy, and volatility. Moreover, the adoption of Tokenomics requires a shift in mindset, from centralized and controlled systems to decentralized and autonomous ones.

Conclusion

In conclusion, the interplay between Tokenomics and traditional economics is complex and multifaceted. While Tokenomics presents a promising new paradigm, it also challenges established economic models and financial systems.

Understanding this interplay is crucial for anyone interested in the future of finance and the blockchain ecosystem.

In the next lesson, we will delve deeper into the concept of token valuation and its importance in Tokenomics.

"The stock market is a device for transferring money from the impatient to the patient."- Warren Buffet

1.8: Introduction to Token Valuation

In this lesson, we will delve into the concept of token valuation, a crucial component of Tokenomics. Token valuation is the process of determining the value of a digital token.

It is an essential aspect of the Tokenomics landscape as it helps investors and traders make informed decisions about buying, selling, or holding a particular token.

Factors Influencing Token Price

Several factors influence the price of a token. Let's explore some of these:

1. **Supply and Demand:** This is the most fundamental factor affecting token price. If the demand for a token exceeds its supply, the price increases. Conversely, if the supply exceeds demand, the price decreases.

2. **Market Sentiment:** The overall mood of investors, often driven by news or social media, can significantly impact token prices. Positive news can lead to price increases, while negative news can cause prices to drop.

3. **Regulatory News:** Announcements of new regulations or changes to existing ones can have a significant impact on token prices. For instance, a government banning cryptocurrencies could lead to a drop in prices.

4. **Technological Developments:** Advances in the underlying technology of a token or its ecosystem can influence its price. For example, a successful software upgrade could lead to price increases.

5. **Token Utility:** If a token has a specific use case or provides a unique service, it can increase its demand, thus raising its price.

Overview of Token Valuation Models

Token valuation models are frameworks used to determine the intrinsic value of a token. Here are a few commonly used models:

1. **Discounted Cash Flow (DCF) Model:** This model is used for tokens that represent an underlying cash flow. The future cash flows are estimated and then discounted back to the present value.

2. **Network Value to Transactions (NVT) Ratio:** This model is like the Price/Earnings ratio in traditional finance. It compares the value of the token's network to the volume of transactions on the network.

3. **Q-Ratio:** This model compares the market price of a token to the cost of replacing all its underlying assets. It is used for tokens that represent a claim on underlying assets.

Challenges and Complexities of Token Valuation

Valuing tokens is a complex task for several reasons

- **Volatility:** Token prices can be highly volatile, making it challenging to determine a stable value.

- **Lack of Fundamental Data:** Unlike traditional assets, tokens often lack fundamental data like cash flows, making it difficult to apply traditional valuation models.

- **Regulatory Uncertainty:** The regulatory landscape for tokens is still evolving, which can create uncertainty and risk.

- **Technological Changes:** Rapid technological changes can quickly make a token obsolete, affecting its value.

In conclusion, understanding token valuation is key to making informed decisions in the Tokenomics landscape. Despite its complexities, it provides valuable insights into the intrinsic value of a token and its potential for future growth.

In the next lesson, we will explore the future of Tokenomics and how it is poised to revolutionize the financial world.

"Do not be obsessed with the price of a stock, be focused on the value of the company." - Peter Lynch

1.9: The Future Of Tokenomics

In this lesson, we will explore the future of Tokenomics, focusing on emerging trends, the potential impact of regulatory changes, and future challenges and opportunities.

Emerging Trends in Tokenomics

Tokenomics is a dynamic field that continues to evolve in response to technological advancements and market needs. Here are some of the most significant emerging trends:

Decentralized Finance (DeFi): DeFi refers to the use of blockchain technology to recreate and improve upon traditional financial systems. DeFi tokens play a crucial role in these systems, serving as a means of exchange, representing value, or earning rewards through liquidity provision or staking.

Decentralized Autonomous Organizations (DAOs):

DAOs are organizations that are run by smart contracts on a blockchain, with token holders voting on decisions. The tokens in DAOs can represent voting rights or a share in the organization's profits.

Non-Fungible Tokens (NFTs): NFTs are unique digital assets that represent ownership of a specific item or piece of content. The rise of NFTs has opened new possibilities for tokenization, including the tokenization of art, real estate, and intellectual property.

Potential Impact of Regulatory Changes on Tokenomics

As the blockchain and cryptocurrency industry matures, it is becoming increasingly subject to regulatory scrutiny. Regulatory changes can have a significant impact on Tokenomics in several ways:

Token Classification: Regulatory bodies around the world are working to classify tokens (as securities, commodities, or something else), which can affect how they are created, distributed, and traded.

Compliance Requirements: As regulators seek to prevent fraud and protect consumers, they may impose new compliance requirements on token issuers and users. These requirements can affect the design of tokens and the systems in which they operate.

Market Access: Regulatory approval can increase market access for certain types of tokens, while regulatory restrictions can limit market access.

Future Challenges and Opportunities in Tokenomics

Looking ahead, Tokenomics faces several challenges and opportunities:

Scalability: As more transactions are conducted using tokens, scalability will become a significant challenge. Solutions such as layer 2 protocols and sharding can help address this issue.

Interoperability: With the proliferation of different blockchains and token standards, interoperability (the ability of different systems to work together) is becoming increasingly important.

Token Utility: As the competition among tokens intensifies, the utility of a token (what you can do with it) will become a key differentiator. Tokens that provide their holders with valuable rights or benefits will likely have an advantage.

Inclusion: One of the most significant opportunities in Tokenomics is the potential to create more inclusive financial systems. By making it easier for people to create, distribute, and trade value, tokens can help to democratize access to financial services.

In conclusion, the future of Tokenomics is likely to be shaped by technological advancements, regulatory changes, and market dynamics. By staying informed about these trends, you can position yourself to take advantage of the opportunities that Tokenomics presents.

"In the cryptocurrency market, the dance of token pricing is a complex ballet, choreographed by supply, demand, utility, and the ever-shifting tides of economic and regulatory currents."
- Dennis Frank

2.1: Understanding Digital Tokens

Introduction to Digital Tokens

Digital tokens, also known as crypto tokens, are a type of virtual currency that represents a particular asset or utility on a blockchain. They are created, distributed, and managed on blockchain technology, which is a decentralized, distributed ledger system. These tokens can represent any asset or utility, such as a unit of value, a stake in a company, or access to a service.

Digital tokens are a fundamental part of the blockchain ecosystem. They are the building blocks of many blockchain-based applications and services.
For example, in a decentralized finance (DeFi) platform, tokens can represent a user's stake in the platform, their voting rights, or the amount of interest they earn.

The Role and Importance of Digital Tokens in the Blockchain Ecosystem

Digital tokens play a crucial role in the blockchain ecosystem. They are used as a medium of exchange, a store of value, and a unit of account in various blockchain networks. They enable the creation of decentralized digital economies and facilitate the exchange of value in a secure, transparent, and efficient manner.

Moreover, digital tokens are instrumental in incentivizing network participants. For instance, miners in the Bitcoin network are rewarded with Bitcoin tokens for validating transactions and adding them to the blockchain. Similarly, in a DeFi lending platform, lenders can earn interest in the form of tokens. Digital tokens also provide a mechanism for the decentralization of governance.

In many blockchain networks, token holders can vote on various network decisions, such as protocol upgrades or changes in network parameters.

This model of governance, known as token-based governance, empowers users and promotes transparency and accountability.

Basic Characteristics of Digital Tokens

Digital tokens exhibit several key characteristics:

1. **Decentralization:** Digital tokens are typically issued and managed on a decentralized network, meaning that no single entity has control over the entire network.

2. **Immutability:** Once a token transaction is validated and added to the blockchain, it cannot be reversed or altered. This ensures the integrity and reliability of token transactions.

3. **Transparency:** All token transactions are recorded on the blockchain and are visible to all network participants. This promotes transparency and helps prevent fraudulent activities.

4. **Interoperability:** Tokens issued on a particular blockchain network can often be used in other networks or platforms, thanks to the interoperability feature of blockchain technology.

5. **Programmability:** Digital tokens can be programmed with specific rules and conditions

using smart contracts. This allows for the creation of complex financial instruments and services.

In conclusion, digital tokens are a pivotal element of the blockchain ecosystem. They serve various functions, from facilitating transactions to enabling decentralized governance, and exhibit unique characteristics that set them apart from traditional forms of currency. Understanding digital tokens is a crucial first step in mastering the field of Tokenomics.

"Far more money has been lost by investors preparing for corrections, or trying to anticipate corrections, than has been lost in corrections themselves." - Peter Lynch

2.2: Utility Tokens

Definition and Purpose of Utility Tokens

Utility tokens, also referred to as app coins or user tokens, represent future access to a company's product or service. The defining characteristic of utility tokens is that they are not created to be an investment. Instead, they are meant to provide users with access to a product or service.

In the blockchain ecosystem, utility tokens are often used as a form of currency within a specific platform or application. They serve a utility function in that they enable users to interact with the platform or use the service. For example, a blockchain-based cloud storage platform might require users to spend utility tokens to buy storage space.

Use Cases and Examples of Utility Tokens

One of the most well-known examples of utility tokens is Ethereum's Ether (ETH). Ether is used to power smart contracts on the Ethereum network, and it also serves as a "fuel" for the network, meaning that users must spend Ether to conduct transactions and execute contracts on the Ethereum platform.

Another example is Filecoin (FIL), a blockchain-based storage network where users can pay in Filecoin tokens to rent hard drive space. Similarly, Basic Attention Token (BAT) is a utility token used in the Brave browser. Users receive BAT tokens for viewing ads, which they can then use to tip content creators or purchase premium content.

Advantages and Disadvantages of Utility Tokens

Advantages:

1. **User Engagement:** Utility tokens can incentivize user engagement and participation within a platform. For instance, users might be encouraged to perform certain actions or behaviors in exchange for tokens.

2. **Fundraising:** Utility tokens can be used as a fundraising tool for start-ups. By selling utility tokens, companies can raise capital to fund the development of their platform or service.

3. **Access to Services:** For users, utility tokens provide access to specific services or features within a platform. This can create a sense of exclusivity or premium access.

Disadvantages:

1. **Regulatory Uncertainty:** The legal status of utility tokens is often unclear, as they can sometimes blur the line between a digital asset and a security. This can lead to potential regulatory challenges.

2. **Market Volatility:** Like other digital assets, the value of utility tokens can be highly volatile. This can pose risks for both users and issuers.

3. **Limited Use:** Utility tokens are typically tied to a specific platform or service, limiting their use to that particular environment.

In conclusion, utility tokens play a crucial role in the blockchain ecosystem by providing a means of access and interaction within specific platforms. However, they also come with their own set of challenges and considerations, particularly in terms of regulatory compliance and market volatility.

As we continue to explore the various types of digital tokens in this course, we will delve deeper into these issues and how they impact the broader landscape of Tokenomics.

"Investing should be more like watching paint dry or watching grass grow. If you want excitement, take $800 and go to Las Vegas." - Paul Samuelson

2.3: Security Tokens

Definition and Purpose of Security Tokens

Security tokens, as their name suggests, are digital assets that derive their value from an external, tradable asset. They are subject to federal laws that govern securities, and non-compliance can result in severe penalties.

The purpose of security tokens is to bring the benefits of blockchain technology, such as transparency, security, and speed, to traditional finance. They provide a bridge between the blockchain world and the traditional finance world.

Security tokens can represent ownership in a company, a share of profits, a voting right, or any other rights that the issuer decides to grant. They are often compared to traditional securities like stocks or bonds because they offer similar rights and benefits.

Security Tokens as Investment Contracts

Security tokens are essentially investment contracts. They represent an agreement between the issuer and the investor, where the investor provides capital with the expectation of future profits in return. The profits can come in various forms, such as dividends, revenue share, or price appreciation of the token.

The Howey Test, a test created by the U.S. Supreme Court, is often used to determine whether a token qualifies as a security. According to the Howey Test, a transaction is an investment contract if:

1. It involves an investment of money.

2. There's an expectation of profits from the investment.

3. The investment of money is in a common enterprise.

31

4. Any profit comes from the efforts of a promoter or third-party.

Use Cases and Examples of Security Tokens

Security tokens can be used in a variety of ways. For instance, they can be used to represent shares in a company, giving holders the right to vote and receive dividends. They can also represent a real estate asset, allowing investors to own a fraction of a property and earn rental income.

One of the most prominent examples of a security token is Blockchain Capital (BCAP). BCAP represents an indirect economic interest in the Blockchain Capital fund, which invests in blockchain-related companies. By purchasing BCAP tokens, investors can participate in the fund's profits.

Another example is tZERO, a platform for trading security tokens. tZERO itself has issued a security token (TZROP), which entitles holders to a share of the company's profits

Regulatory Considerations for Security Tokens

Given their nature, security tokens are subject to securities regulations. In the U.S., for example, they must comply with the Securities Act of 1933 and the Securities Exchange Act of 1934.

These laws require issuers to register securities with the Securities and Exchange Commission (SEC) unless an exemption applies. Issuers must also provide accurate and comprehensive information about their operations, financial condition, and risk factors. Furthermore, they must take measures to prevent money laundering and ensure investor protection.

In conclusion, security tokens offer a way to bring the benefits of blockchain technology to traditional finance. However, they also come with regulatory challenges that issuers must carefully navigate. As the regulatory landscape evolves, we can expect to see more innovative uses of security tokens in the future.

2.4: Governance Tokens

Definition and Purpose of Governance Tokens

Governance tokens are a type of digital token that grant holders the right to vote on changes to a platform's protocol, rules, or decision-making process. They are a critical component of Decentralized Autonomous Organizations (DAOs) and other decentralized platforms, where they serve as a means of achieving consensus among users.

Unlike utility tokens, which are used to access a specific product or service within a platform, or security tokens, which represent an underlying asset, governance tokens do not confer any direct economic benefits. Instead, their value lies in the influence they grant over the platform's future development and direction.

The Role of Governance Tokens in Decentralized Autonomous Organizations (DAOs)

In a DAO, governance tokens play an essential role in decision-making processes. DAOs are organizations that are run by smart contracts on a blockchain, with no central authority.

Instead, decisions are made collectively by the community through a voting system, where each vote's weight is proportional to the number of governance tokens held by a user.

This system ensures that the control and future direction of the DAO are in the hands of those who use it or are otherwise invested in its success. It also promotes transparency and accountability, as all decisions are recorded on the blockchain and can be audited by anyone.

Use Cases and Examples of Governance Tokens

There are numerous examples of governance tokens in use today. Here are a few notable ones:

Uniswap (UNI): Uniswap is a decentralized exchange protocol built on the Ethereum blockchain. UNI tokens are used to vote on changes to the protocol, such as fee structures or the introduction of new features.

Compound (COMP): Compound is a decentralized lending platform, also built on Ethereum. COMP token holders can propose and vote on changes to the platform, including interest rates and collateral requirements.

Aave (AAVE): Aave is a decentralized money market protocol where users can lend and borrow cryptocurrencies. AAVE tokens are used to vote on changes to the platform's rules and parameters.

In each of these cases, the governance token serves as a means of decentralizing control and promoting community involvement in the platform's development. This approach aligns with the broader ethos of the blockchain and cryptocurrency space, which values decentralization, transparency, and community governance.

In summary, governance tokens are a powerful tool for decentralization and community engagement in blockchain platforms. They allow users to have a say in the platforms they use, fostering a sense of ownership and commitment that can be beneficial for the platform's long-term success. As the blockchain space continues to evolve, the role and importance of governance tokens are likely to grow.

"Speculation is most dangerous when it looks easiest." - Warren Buffet

2.5: Non-Fungible Tokens (NFTs)

Understanding the Uniqueness of NFTs

Non-Fungible Tokens (NFTs) are a special type of digital token that represent unique assets. Unlike fungible tokens such as Bitcoin or Ethereum, which are identical to each other and can be exchanged on a one-for-one basis, NFTs are unique and cannot be exchanged on a like-for-like basis. This uniqueness and scarcity are what give NFTs their value.

NFTs are created using a standard called ERC-721 on the Ethereum blockchain. This standard allows for the creation of tokens with unique attributes, making them ideal for representing ownership of unique items or assets.

Each NFT has a distinct value and specific information that separates it from other tokens. This information is stored on the blockchain, providing transparency, and proving ownership.

Use Cases and Examples of NFTs

NFTs have a wide range of use cases, from digital art and music to virtual real estate and virtual goods in video games. Here are a few examples:

Digital Art: Digital artists can create artwork as NFTs and sell them directly to consumers, eliminating the need for intermediaries. The NFT contains provable ownership of the artwork, and artists can also program royalties into the NFT to receive a percentage of sales whenever the artwork is sold to a new owner. A notable example is the digital artist Beeple, whose NFT artwork sold for $69 million at Christie's auction house.

Virtual Real Estate: Virtual worlds like Decentraland and Cryptovoxels allow users to buy, sell, and trade virtual land and property as NFTs. These virtual properties can be developed and monetized, like real-world real estate.

Collectibles: NFTs have given rise to a new form of collectibles. CryptoKitties, one of the first NFT games, allows players to buy, sell, and breed unique virtual cats.

The Impact of NFTs on Art and Collectibles

NFTs are revolutionizing the art and collectibles industry in several ways:

Democratizing Art Ownership: NFTs allow digital artists to sell their work directly to the public. This opens art ownership to a broader audience who may not have access to traditional art markets.

Provable Ownership: NFTs use blockchain technology to prove ownership and authenticity of the artwork. This helps to prevent forgery and provides transparency in the art market.

Royalties for Artists: NFTs can be programmed to pay royalties to artists whenever their work is resold. This provides ongoing income for artists, which is not typically the case in the traditional art market.

In conclusion, NFTs are a groundbreaking innovation in the world of digital tokens. They represent a significant shift in how we perceive the value and ownership of digital assets. As we continue to explore the potential of blockchain technology, the impact and use cases of NFTs are expected to expand even further.

2.6: Other Types of Tokens

In this lesson, we will explore some other types of tokens that play a significant role in the blockchain ecosystem. These include payment tokens and equity tokens. We will delve into their definitions and use cases and compare them with the tokens we have previously discussed.

Introduction to Other Types of Tokens

Payment Tokens

Payment tokens are a type of digital token that are primarily used as a medium of exchange in the blockchain ecosystem.

They are like traditional currencies but operate on a decentralized blockchain network. Bitcoin is the most popular example of a payment token. It was designed to facilitate peer-to-peer transactions without the need for a central authority like a bank.

Equity Tokens

Equity tokens represent ownership in an underlying asset, like shares in a company. These tokens democratize access to capital and can be a powerful tool for startups and small businesses that want to raise funds.

They are often issued through a Security Token Offering (STO), which is subject to securities regulations. An example of an equity token is the Blockchain Capital (BCAP) token, which represents an indirect fractional non-voting economic interest in Blockchain Capital's venture capital fund.

Use Cases and Examples of These Tokens

Payment tokens like Bitcoin are used for transactions, both online and offline. They are accepted by a growing number of merchants worldwide.

Other use cases include remittances, where payment tokens can facilitate faster and cheaper international money transfers.

Equity tokens, on the other hand, are used for fundraising and capital formation. They can represent a claim on a company's assets and earnings.

They also enable fractional ownership, which can make previously illiquid assets like real estate or art more accessible to the average investor.

Comparing and Contrasting Different Types of Tokens

Each type of token has its unique features and use cases. For instance, utility tokens provide access to a specific product or service within a blockchain ecosystem. In contrast, security tokens represent an investment contract and derive their value from an external asset.

Payment tokens, as we have seen, are used as a medium of exchange. They are often more volatile than traditional currencies due to the nascent and speculative nature of the crypto market.

Equity tokens are like traditional shares but operate on a blockchain. They can provide more transparency and efficiency than traditional securities, thanks to the inherent properties of blockchain technology.

In the next lesson, we will explore token standards, which provide a set of rules for tokens to follow within their respective blockchain ecosystems. This ensures that the tokens can interact seamlessly with each other and with other elements of the blockchain infrastructure.

2.7: Token Standards

Understanding Token Standards

Token standards are a set of rules that dictate how tokens can be created, transferred, and interacted within a blockchain ecosystem. These standards are fundamental to ensuring that tokens can be easily understood, utilized, and integrated across different platforms and applications. Two of the most popular token standards within the Ethereum blockchain are ERC-20 and ERC-721.

ERC-20

ERC-20, or Ethereum Request for Comment 20, is the standard for fungible tokens on the Ethereum blockchain. Fungible tokens are interchangeable with each other, much like traditional fiat currencies.

This standard outlines a set of rules and functions that a token must adhere to and implement, including how tokens are transferred, how to access data about a token, and how to manage token ownership.

ERC-721

ERC-721, on the other hand, is a standard for non-fungible tokens (NFTs). Unlike ERC-20 tokens, ERC-721 tokens are unique and not interchangeable. This uniqueness and scarcity are what give NFTs their value. NFTs can represent ownership over digital or physical assets, from digital art and music to real estate and more.

The Role of Token Standards in Interoperability and Functionality

Token standards play a crucial role in promoting interoperability and functionality within the blockchain ecosystem. Interoperability refers to the ability of computer systems or software to exchange and make use of information. In the context of blockchain, it means that tokens following the same standard can interact seamlessly with each other.

For instance, an ERC-20 token can be easily exchanged with another ERC-20 token within the Ethereum ecosystem. This interoperability extends to decentralized applications (DApps) built on Ethereum, which can easily integrate and interact with ERC-20 tokens.

In terms of functionality, token standards ensure that tokens behave in a predictable manner. This predictability allows developers to build applications that can interact with a variety of tokens without needing to understand the intricacies of each token's code. For example, a digital wallet can support any ERC-20 token because all ERC-20 tokens follow the same set of rules.

Differences Between Various Token Standards

While there are many token standards, the key differences lie in their use cases and the rules they enforce. ERC-20, as mentioned earlier, is used for fungible tokens and is the most common standard for issuing tokens in Initial Coin Offerings (ICOs).

ERC-721, conversely, is used for non-fungible tokens, which are unique and can represent ownership over a wide range of assets. Other standards like ERC-223, ERC-777, and ERC-1155 introduce additional functionality, improved security, and increased efficiency.

In conclusion, understanding token standards is crucial for anyone interested in Tokenomics. These standards not only dictate how tokens are created and interacted with but also play a significant role in ensuring interoperability and functionality within the blockchain ecosystem.

2.8: Token Use Cases Across Industries

In this lesson, we will explore the various ways digital tokens are utilized across different industries. We will examine real-world examples of token usage in sectors such as finance, supply chain, gaming, and more. We will also discuss the future potential and emerging trends in token use across industries.

Exploring How Different Types of Tokens are Used Across Various Industries

Digital tokens have found their way into various industries, each with unique applications and benefits. Let's delve into some of these sectors and how they are leveraging tokens:

Finance: In the financial sector, tokens are often used to represent assets or ownership rights. Security tokens, for instance, can represent shares in a company, while stablecoins can be pegged to real-world assets like fiat currency or gold. Decentralized finance (DeFi) also heavily relies on tokens for various functionalities such as lending, borrowing, and yield farming.

Supply Chain: Tokens can help enhance transparency and traceability in supply chains. For example, a token can represent a specific product, and its movement through the supply chain can be tracked on the blockchain, ensuring authenticity, and preventing fraud.

Gaming: In the gaming industry, tokens can represent in-game assets, such as characters, items, or currency. Non-fungible tokens (NFTs) have been particularly popular in this space, allowing players to truly own their digital assets and even trade them in secondary markets.

41

Real-World Examples of Token Use in Industries

Let's look at some real-world examples of token use across these industries:

Finance: MakerDAO, a DeFi platform, uses its native token, MKR, for governance and DAI as a stablecoin pegged to the US dollar. Users can lend and borrow DAI, while MKR holders can vote on important decisions in the ecosystem.

Supply Chain: VeChain uses its VET and VTHO tokens to track products in a supply chain. Each product is assigned a unique ID, represented by a token, which can be tracked on the VeChain blockchain.

Gaming: CryptoKitties, a blockchain-based game, uses NFTs to represent unique digital cats that players can breed, collect, and sell.

Future Potential and Emerging Trends in Token Use Across Industries

The use of tokens across industries is still in its early stages, and we can expect to see many more innovative applications in the future. Some emerging trends include:

Tokenization of Real-World Assets: More and more real-world assets, from real estate to art, are being tokenized, allowing for fractional ownership and increased liquidity.

Governance Tokens: As more platforms move towards decentralized governance, we can expect to see an increase in the use of governance tokens, which allow holders to vote on decisions within the ecosystem.

Interoperability: As the blockchain space matures, we can expect to see more interoperability between different blockchains and their respective tokens, allowing for more complex and integrated applications of the role of tokens in Decentralized Finance (DeFi).

"An investment in knowledge pays
the best interest."
- Benjamin Franklin

2.9: The Role of Tokens in Decentralized Finance (DeFi)

In this lesson, we will recap the diverse types of digital tokens that we have discussed so far, look at some emerging trends, and discuss the outlook for digital tokens. We will also consider the potential impact of regulatory changes on different types of tokens.

Recap of Digital Tokens and Their Use Cases

Throughout this module, we have delved into various types of digital tokens, each with their unique characteristics and use cases.

- **Utility Tokens:** These tokens provide access to a product or service within a blockchain ecosystem. They are not designed as investments, but their value can increase as the demand for the product or service rises.

- **Security Tokens:** These tokens derive their value from an external, tradable asset and are subject to federal securities regulations. They represent ownership in an underlying asset and have the potential to yield profits.

- **Governance Tokens:** These tokens allow holders to vote on decisions within a blockchain ecosystem, providing a level of control and influence over the project's direction.

- **Non-Fungible Tokens (NFTs):** These tokens represent ownership of unique items or pieces of content. Unlike other tokens, NFTs are not interchangeable as each has a distinct value.

Emerging Trends and Future Outlook for Digital Tokens

The digital token landscape is rapidly evolving, with new types of tokens emerging and existing ones finding new applications. Here are some trends to watch:

- **Interoperability:** As blockchain ecosystems grow, there is an increasing need for different types of tokens to interact seamlessly. We can expect more tokens designed for interoperability in the future.

- **Tokenization of Real-World Assets:** From real estate to art, the tokenization of tangible assets is a trend that is likely to continue. This trend could broaden the scope of digital tokens beyond the digital realm.

- **Decentralized Finance (DeFi):** DeFi is a major driver of innovation in the token space. As this sector continues to grow, we can expect to see more tokens tied to DeFi services.

The Potential Impact of Regulatory Changes on Different Types of Tokens

Regulation is a significant factor that can influence the future of digital tokens. As governments around the world grapple with how to regulate cryptocurrencies, these decisions will inevitably impact token ecosystems.

- **Utility Tokens:** Regulatory clarity could lead to an increase in utility tokens, as businesses will have a clearer framework for launching these tokens without fear of regulatory backlash.

- **Security Tokens:** As these tokens are already subject to securities regulations, further regulatory clarity could help streamline the process of launching security tokens and attract more traditional investors to the space.

- **Governance Tokens and NFTs:** The regulatory future for these tokens is still uncertain. However, as they gain popularity, we can expect regulators to pay more attention to them.

In conclusion, the future of digital tokens is bright, but not without challenges. As we navigate this evolving landscape, staying informed and adaptable will be key to success.

"Supply and demand are the scissors of price." -Alfred Marshall

3.1: Introduction to Token Creation and Distribution Mechanisms

Understanding the Role of Token Creation and Distribution in Tokenomics

Token creation and distribution are fundamental aspects of Tokenomics. They form the backbone of any cryptocurrency project, determining how tokens are generated and disseminated among participants in the ecosystem.

The way tokens are created and distributed can significantly impact the overall functionality of the token, its value, and its perception in the market.

In essence, token creation is the process of generating new tokens within a blockchain ecosystem. The rules of token creation are often coded into the blockchain protocol itself.
These rules dictate the total supply of tokens, the rate of new token creation, and the conditions under which new tokens are generated.

Distribution, on the other hand, refers to the process of allocating these created tokens to participants within the ecosystem. This could be through various mechanisms such as Initial Coin Offerings (ICOs), Security Token Offerings (STOs), Airdrops, Forks, mining, staking, and more.

The distribution process is crucial as it determines who gets to own the tokens and in what quantity, thereby influencing the decentralization and security of the network.

The Lifecycle of a Digital Token from Creation to Distribution

The lifecycle of a digital token can be broadly divided into two phases: creation and distribution.

1. **Creation:** This is the initial phase where the token is conceptualized and then created. The token's purpose, total supply, and rules for creation are defined at this stage. The token is then coded and launched on a blockchain platform.

2. **Distribution**: Once the token is created, the next phase is to distribute it to the participants in the network. The method of distribution can vary based on the project's goals and the type of token.

   For instance, tokens can be distributed through public sales like ICOs or STOs, given as rewards for mining or staking, or distributed via airdrops.

Different Methods of Token Creation and Distribution

There are several methods for token creation and distribution, each with its own set of advantages, disadvantages, and use cases. Here are a few common methods:

1. **Initial Coin Offerings (ICOs):** ICOs are public sales of tokens, where the project team sells a portion of the tokens to early investors. The funds raised through an ICO are typically used to develop the project further.

2. **Security Token Offerings (STOs):** STOs are like ICOs, but the tokens sold represent an underlying asset or a share in the company, making them subject to securities regulations.

3. **Airdrops:** Airdrops are a method of distributing tokens for free to holders of a particular blockchain currency, such as Bitcoin or Ethereum. Airdrops are often used for marketing purposes or to reward loyal customers.

4. **Forks:** Forks are a method of creating new tokens by modifying the existing code of a blockchain. The new tokens are often distributed to holders of the original blockchain's currency.

5. **Mining and Staking:** In some blockchain networks, new tokens are created and distributed as rewards for mining or staking. Mining involves solving complex mathematical problems to validate transactions and secure the network, while staking involves holding and locking up a certain number of tokens to validate transactions.

In the next lessons, we will delve deeper into each of these methods, exploring their intricacies, benefits, drawbacks, and real-world applications.

3.2: Initial Coin Offerings (ICOs)

Understanding the Concept of ICOs

An Initial Coin Offering (ICO) is a fundraising mechanism in the blockchain world, akin to an Initial Public Offering (IPO) in the traditional finance sector. However, unlike IPOs, ICOs offer digital tokens instead of shares in a company.

These tokens can represent various utilities or rights within the blockchain ecosystem of a project and are typically purchased with existing cryptocurrencies, most commonly Bitcoin or Ethereum.

ICOs emerged as a revolutionary and democratized way of raising capital, enabling startups to bypass traditional fundraising methods and directly reach out to potential investors or users worldwide.

The Process of Launching an ICO

Launching an ICO involves several steps:

1. **Whitepaper Publication:** The project team publishes a whitepaper detailing the project's concept, technology, token utility, team members, roadmap, and details of the ICO, including token price, ICO date, and distribution plan.

2. **Marketing and Promotion:** The team undertakes marketing efforts to create awareness and generate interest in the ICO. This could involve social media campaigns, partnerships, and community building.

3. **Token Sale:** During the ICO, interested participants purchase the tokens using cryptocurrencies. The sale could be open to all or restricted to approved participants, depending on the project's regulatory compliance needs.

4. **Token Distribution:** After the ICO, the tokens are distributed to the participants' blockchain addresses.

5. **Listing on Exchanges:** Post-ICO, the token is usually listed on cryptocurrency exchanges to provide liquidity to token holders.

Advantages and Disadvantages of ICOs

Advantages:

Democratization of Investment: ICOs allow anyone worldwide to invest in a project, democratizing access to investment opportunities.

Liquidity: Tokens can be sold or bought on cryptocurrency exchanges, providing liquidity to investors.

Potential for High Returns: Some ICOs have provided astronomical returns to early investors, although such cases are exceptions rather than the norm.

Disadvantages:

Regulatory Risk: ICOs have faced scrutiny from regulators worldwide due to concerns about investor protection, given the high risk and lack of regulatory oversight.

Scams and Frauds: The ICO space has seen numerous scams and fraudulent projects that have resulted in significant losses for investors.

Market Volatility: The value of tokens can be highly volatile, leading to potential losses for investors.

Case Studies of Successful and Failed ICOs

Successful ICO: Ethereum

Ethereum's ICO in 2014 is one of the most successful ICOs ever. It raised $18 million in Bitcoin, and the Ethereum token (ETH) has since become the second-largest cryptocurrency by market capitalization.

Failed ICO: The DAO

The DAO (Decentralized Autonomous Organization) raised $150 million in its 2016 ICO but was soon hacked, leading to a loss of around $50 million. The incident resulted in a hard fork of Ethereum and has since served as a cautionary tale in the crypto community.

In conclusion, ICOs have been a game-changer in fundraising, but they come with their own set of challenges and risks. Understanding these aspects is crucial for anyone planning to participate in an ICO or launch one.

3.3: Security Token Offerings (STOs)

Introduction to STOs and How They Differ from ICOs

Security Token Offerings (STOs) are a type of public offering in which tokenized digital securities, known as security tokens, are sold in cryptocurrency exchanges, or security token exchanges. These tokens represent underlying real-world assets such as real estate, stocks, or bonds.

Unlike Initial Coin Offerings (ICOs), which may not necessarily represent a stake in a company, STOs provide investors with an equity stake in the company issuing the tokens.

STOs are often seen as a hybrid approach between cryptocurrency ICOs and the more traditional Initial Public Offering (IPO) because they offer the benefits of blockchain technology along with the legal safeguards of traditional securities.

The Regulatory Landscape for STOs

STOs are subject to federal securities regulations, which makes them different from ICOs. This regulatory oversight aims to protect investors and give them a level of assurance that the offering is legitimate, and the company has met certain criteria.

Regulations vary by country, but in general, STOs must comply with securities laws, including registering with regulatory bodies and providing detailed information about their operations, financial status, and risk factors. In the United States, for example, STOs must comply with the Securities and Exchange Commission (SEC) regulations.

The Process of Launching an STO

Launching an STO involves several steps. First, the company must decide what assets or part of their business they wish to tokenize. This could be equity in the company, real estate, or any other asset that can be legally owned.

Next, the company must collaborate with legal counsel to ensure they are in compliance with all relevant securities laws. This includes registering the STO with regulatory bodies and preparing a prospectus that details the offering.

Once the legal groundwork has been laid, the company can then develop the security tokens. This involves creating a smart contract on a blockchain that represents the security token and dictates the rules of the token (such as who can own it and how it can be transferred).

Finally, the company can launch the STO, either on its own platform or through a third-party platform. Investors can then purchase the tokens, typically using cryptocurrency.

Case Studies of Successful STOs

Several companies have successfully launched STOs. For example, in 2018, the blockchain-based real estate platform Propy conducted an STO for a real estate property in California. The STO was fully compliant with SEC regulations and marked one of the first times a real property was tokenized on the blockchain.

Another example is tZERO, a subsidiary of Overstock.com, which launched an STO in 2018. The tZERO STO was one of the largest to date, raising over $134 million.

These case studies demonstrate the potential of STOs as a fundraising tool that combines the benefits of blockchain with the regulatory safeguards of traditional securities.

In conclusion, STOs represent an evolution in the way companies can raise funds and investors can participate in offerings.

By offering a level of regulatory oversight not typically found in ICOs, STOs provide a more secure and legally compliant way to invest in blockchain-based projects.

However, like all investments, STOs come with risks, and potential investors should always conduct thorough due diligence before participating in an STO.

"Beware of little expenses. A small leak will sink a great ship."
- Benjamin Franklin

3.4: Airdrops as a Distribution Mechanism

Understanding the Concept of Airdrops in Token Distribution

An airdrop is a popular method used by blockchain projects to distribute tokens to the wallets of some users free of charge. Airdrops are usually used by blockchain-based startups to bootstrap their cryptocurrency projects.

Their primary purpose is to spread awareness about the project and to get the maximum number of people to start using the tokens.

The Strategic Importance of Airdrops in Marketing and User Acquisition

Airdrops serve as a vital marketing tool in the blockchain industry. They are an excellent way to create buzz and interest in a new project. By offering free tokens, projects can attract a large user base and incentivize them to use the tokens within their ecosystem.

This strategy helps to increase the token's visibility, credibility, and market value. Moreover, airdrops can also be used to reward loyal customers or to attract new users to a platform. For instance, a project may decide to airdrop tokens to all wallet addresses that hold a particular amount of a specific token.

The Process of Conducting an Airdrop

The process of conducting an airdrop involves several steps:

- **Announcement**: The project team announces the airdrop to the public, detailing the criteria for participation, the number of tokens to be distributed, and the date of the airdrop.

- **Participant Selection**: Depending on the criteria set by the project team, some airdrops may require users to perform certain tasks, like sharing posts on social media or signing up for newsletters. Other airdrops may distribute tokens to users who hold a certain amount of the project's tokens or a specific cryptocurrency like Bitcoin or Ethereum.

- **Distribution**: Once the participants are selected, the tokens are automatically deposited into their wallets. The distribution process can be instant or may take some time, depending on the project.

Case Studies of Successful Airdrops

One of the most successful examples of an airdrop is the **Uniswap (UNI) airdrop**. In September 2020, Uniswap, a decentralized exchange, airdropped 400 UNI tokens to every wallet that had interacted with the platform before September 1, 2020.

At the time of the airdrop, these tokens were worth around $1,200, and the price has since significantly increased, making it one of the most lucrative airdrops in history.

Another successful airdrop was conducted by **Stellar Lumens (XLM)**. In 2019, Stellar partnered with Blockchain.com to airdrop $125 million worth of XLM tokens to the Blockchain.com users.

Airdrops have proven to be an effective strategy for token distribution, marketing, and user acquisition.

However, it's essential for users to stay vigilant as there are also fraudulent schemes that disguise themselves as airdrops. Always do your research before participating in an airdrop.

In the next section, we will discuss another important aspect of token creation and distribution - Forks.

"Know what you own and know why you own it." - Peter Lynch

3.5: Forks in Token Creation and Distribution

In this lesson, we will delve into the concept of forks in the blockchain and their role in token creation and distribution. We will differentiate between hard forks and soft forks and explore some significant forks in the cryptocurrency space through case studies.

Understanding the Concept of Forks in Blockchain

A fork in the blockchain is a divergence in the protocol or rules governing the blockchain network. It usually happens when these rules need to be changed or upgraded. Forks can lead to the creation of a new blockchain that splits off from the original one, and in the process, new tokens may be created and distributed.

The Role of Forks in Token Creation and Distribution

Forks play a critical role in token creation and distribution. When a fork occurs, all the existing users of the old blockchain get the new tokens in the new blockchain. This distribution is usually in a 1:1 ratio, meaning for every token a user held in the old blockchain, they receive one token in the new blockchain.

Differentiating Between Hard Forks and Soft Forks

There are two types of forks: hard forks and soft forks.

Hard Forks: A hard fork is a radical change to the protocol that makes previously invalid transactions or blocks valid, or vice versa. It requires all nodes or users to upgrade to the latest version of the protocol software.

It can result in a permanent divergence from the original blockchain if not enough users upgrade to the new version, leading to the creation of a new blockchain and new tokens. Examples of hard forks include Bitcoin Cash and Ethereum Classic.

Soft Forks: A soft fork, on the other hand, is a backward-compatible change to the protocol. This means that even non-upgraded nodes can still validate transactions.

However, they will not recognize the new rules and will continue to operate under the old rules. Soft forks do not result in new tokens or a new blockchain.

Case Studies of Significant Forks in the Cryptocurrency Space

Let's look at two significant hard forks that resulted in the creation and distribution of new tokens.

Bitcoin Cash (BCH): In 2017, Bitcoin underwent a hard fork that resulted in the creation of Bitcoin Cash. The fork was initiated due to disagreements within the Bitcoin community about how to scale the network. Those who forked to Bitcoin Cash wanted to increase the block size from 1MB to 8MB to accommodate more transactions per block.

Ethereum Classic (ETC): Ethereum Classic is a result of a hard fork from the original Ethereum blockchain. The fork occurred following the DAO attack in 2016, where $50 million worth of Ether was stolen.

The Ethereum community decided to hard fork the blockchain to return the stolen funds, but some members disagreed with this decision, leading to the creation of Ethereum Classic. In conclusion, forks in blockchain play a vital role in token creation and distribution.

They allow for the evolution and improvement of blockchain networks and, in the process, can create new opportunities for traders and investors.

In the next lesson, we will explore other distribution strategies used in Tokenomics.

3.6: Other Distribution Strategies

In this lesson, we will explore other token distribution strategies beyond ICOs, STOs, Airdrops, and Forks. These strategies include mining, staking, and yield farming.

We will also compare these distribution strategies and their use cases and understand their role in the overall token economy. Finally, we will analyze case studies of the successful use of these distribution strategies.

Mining

Mining is one of the earliest forms of token distribution. In the context of cryptocurrencies, mining involves validating new transactions and recording them on the global ledger.

For their efforts, miners are rewarded with new tokens. This distribution strategy is commonly used by cryptocurrencies like Bitcoin and Ethereum.

Staking

Staking is another popular token distribution strategy. It involves holding tokens in a cryptocurrency wallet to support the operations of a blockchain network. These operations can include validating transactions or maintaining the network's security.

In return for staking their tokens, participants may receive additional tokens as rewards. This strategy is commonly used in Proof-of-Stake (PoS) and Delegated Proof-of-Stake (DPoS) blockchain networks.

Yield Farming

Yield farming, also known as liquidity mining, is a relatively new token distribution strategy. It involves lending your tokens to others through smart contracts. In return, lenders earn fees or additional tokens. This strategy has been popularized by

Decentralized Finance (DeFi) platforms like Compound and Uniswap.

Comparing Distribution Strategies

Each distribution strategy has its own set of benefits and drawbacks. Mining, for instance, provides a fair way of distributing tokens but can be resource intensive.

Staking, on the other hand, encourages token holders to participate in the network but can lead to centralization. Yield farming can provide high returns but also comes with high risks.

Role in the Token Economy

These distribution strategies play a crucial role in the token economy. They incentivize participation in the network, maintain the network's security, and facilitate the distribution of tokens in a decentralized manner. They also influence the supply and demand dynamics of the token, which can impact the token's price.

Case Studies

Let's look at a couple of case studies. Bitcoin, the first cryptocurrency, uses mining as its primary distribution strategy. This has allowed it to maintain a decentralized network of miners who validate transactions and secure the network.

On the other hand, EOS uses a Delegated Proof-of-Stake (DPoS) model, where token holders vote for delegates who validate transactions and maintain the network. This staking model has allowed EOS to achieve faster transaction times compared to Bitcoin.

In the DeFi space, Compound has popularized yield farming by allowing users to earn COMP tokens in return for lending or borrowing on the platform. This has led to a significant increase in the platform's total value locked (TVL).

In conclusion, understanding these token distribution strategies is crucial for anyone involved in the token economy. They not only determine how tokens are distributed but also influence the overall functionality and success of the blockchain network.

"Successful investing is about managing risk, not avoiding it."
- Benjamin Graham

3.7: Legal and Regulatory Considerations in Token Creation

Understanding the Legal Landscape for Token Creation and Distribution

In the world of Tokenomics, understanding the legal landscape is crucial for the successful creation and distribution of tokens. Countries around the world have different legal frameworks and regulations concerning digital tokens.

For instance, some countries like Switzerland and Malta have relatively friendly regulations, while others like China and India have stricter rules. It's important to familiarize yourself with the legal environment in your target markets before embarking on a token creation and distribution project.

Compliance Requirements for Different Distribution Strategies

Different token distribution strategies have varying compliance requirements. For instance, Initial Coin Offerings (ICOs) and Security Token Offerings (STOs) are subject to different regulations. ICOs, which are often used to raise funds for projects in the early stages, have faced criticism for their lack of regulatory oversight.

On the other hand, STOs, which involve the issuance of securities tokens that represent ownership in an underlying asset, are subject to securities laws in many jurisdictions.

Airdrops, another popular distribution strategy, involves the free distribution of tokens to holders of a particular blockchain currency. While this method can be an effective way to distribute tokens and generate interest, it can also raise legal issues, particularly if the tokens are considered securities.

The Role of Regulatory Bodies in Token Distribution

Regulatory bodies play a crucial role in overseeing token distribution. In the United States, for example, the Securities and Exchange Commission (SEC) has taken action against several ICOs for violating securities laws.

Similarly, in Europe, the European Securities and Markets Authority (ESMA) provides guidelines for token distribution, particularly for STOs.

Regulatory bodies seek to protect investors, maintain fair, orderly, and efficient markets, and facilitate capital formation. They can impose fines and sanctions, and in some cases, they can halt token sales or distributions that violate laws.

Case Studies of Regulatory Interventions in Token Distribution

There have been several notable cases of regulatory interventions in token distribution. One of the most well-known is the SEC's action against Telegram's $1.7 billion ICO.

The SEC argued that Telegram's token was a security, and as such, it should have been registered with the commission. Ultimately, Telegram had to return funds to investors and pay a penalty.

Another case involved the blockchain company Block.one, which conducted the EOS ICO. The SEC ordered Block.one to pay a $24 million penalty for conducting an unregistered securities sale.

These cases highlight the importance of understanding and complying with regulations when creating and distributing tokens.

In conclusion, legal and regulatory considerations are a critical aspect of Tokenomics. Compliance with laws and regulations not only helps protect investors but also contributes to the legitimacy and credibility of the token and the project behind it.

As the regulatory landscape continues to evolve, staying updated with the latest developments is crucial for anyone involved in token creation and distribution.

"Tokenomics weaves a tapestry of trust with threads of transparency, driven by the loom of ledger technology." - Dennis Frank

3.8: Best Practices and Pitfalls in Token Creation and Distribution

Introduction

In this lesson, we'll delve into the best practices and pitfalls in token creation and distribution. We'll discuss strategies to overcome these challenges and look at case studies of successful and failed token distribution strategies.

Best Practices in Token Creation and Distribution

1. **Clear Purpose and Utility**: Tokens should have a clear purpose and utility within their respective ecosystems. This not only helps in attracting potential investors but also in maintaining the token's value over time.

2. **Transparent Communication**: Transparency is key in any token creation and distribution process. Providing clear, consistent, and regular updates to the community can build trust and credibility.

3. **Legal Compliance**: Ensure that the token creation and distribution process comply with relevant laws and regulations. This can help avoid potential legal issues down the line.

4. **Security Measures**: Implement robust security measures to protect against potential threats. This includes using secure smart contract platforms and conducting thorough security audits.

5. **Fair Distribution Mechanism**: A fair and transparent distribution mechanism can help ensure that tokens are distributed evenly and not concentrated in the hands of a few.

Common Pitfalls and Challenges in Token Distribution

- **Lack of Transparency**: Lack of transparency can lead to mistrust and skepticism among potential investors.

- **Regulatory Uncertainty**: The regulatory landscape for tokens is still evolving, and non-compliance can lead to legal issues.

- **Poor Security Measures**: Poor security measures can make the token susceptible to hacks and other security threats.

- **Lack of Utility**: Tokens with no apparent utility or purpose can struggle to maintain their value over time.

- **Unfair Distribution**: An unfair distribution mechanism can lead to a concentration of tokens in the hands of a few, leading to centralization and potential manipulation.

Strategies to Overcome These Challenges

- **Transparency**: Be transparent about the token's purpose, utility, and distribution mechanism. Regularly communicate updates to the community.

- **Legal Compliance**: Stay updated with the latest regulatory developments and ensure compliance.

- **Robust Security Measures**: Implement robust security measures and conduct regular security audits.

- **Clear Utility**: Ensure the token has a clear utility within its ecosystem.

- **Fair Distribution Mechanism**: Implement a fair and transparent distribution mechanism.

Case Studies

Successful Token Distribution: Ethereum

Ethereum's token distribution through its Initial Coin Offering (ICO) in 2014 is often cited as a successful example.

The Ethereum team was transparent about the token's utility and distribution mechanism. They also complied with relevant laws and regulations and implemented robust security measures.

Failed Token Distribution: The DAO

The DAO (Decentralized Autonomous Organization) is an example of a failed token distribution. Despite raising a significant amount of funds in its ICO,

The DAO was hacked due to poor security measures. This led to a loss of investor confidence and eventually, the dissolution of The DAO.

Conclusion

Understanding the best practices and pitfalls in token creation and distribution is crucial for anyone planning to launch their own digital tokens.

By learning from the successes and failures of past projects, we can navigate the complex landscape of tokenomics more effectively.

In the next lesson, we'll explore the future of token creation and distribution.

Quiz Question: What are some of the best practices in token creation and distribution?

Quiz Answer: Clear Purpose and Utility, Transparent Communication, Legal Compliance, Security Measures, Fair Distribution Mechanism.

Quiz Question: What are some common pitfalls in token distribution?

Quiz Answer: Lack of Transparency, Regulatory Uncertainty, Poor Security Measures, Lack of Utility, Unfair Distribution.

Quiz Question: What can we learn from the case studies of Ethereum and The DAO?

Quiz Answer: The importance of transparency, legal compliance, robust security measures, clear utility, and a fair distribution mechanism in token creation and distribution.

3.9: The Future of Token Creation and Distribution

Introduction

In this lesson, we will explore the future of token creation and distribution. We will delve into emerging trends, the impact of technological advancements, and predictions for the future. We will also discuss how to prepare for these future changes.

Emerging Trends in Token Creation and Distribution

The token creation and distribution landscape are continuously evolving, with new trends emerging regularly. One such trend is the rise of Decentralized Finance (DeFi), which has led to the creation of a multitude of new tokens. These tokens often have unique distribution mechanisms, such as liquidity mining, where users earn tokens by providing liquidity to a protocol.

Another trend is the increasing use of DAOs (Decentralized Autonomous Organizations) in token distribution. DAOs allow for a more democratic distribution process, as token holders can vote on various aspects of the distribution process. Moreover, the concept of Fair Launch is gaining traction.

In a Fair Launch, there is no pre-mine, pre-sale, or allocation to the team. All tokens are distributed to the community, often through liquidity mining or yield farming.

The Impact of Technological Advancements on Token Distribution

Technological advancements are significantly impacting token distribution. The rise of blockchain technology and smart contracts has made it possible to automate the distribution process, reducing the need for intermediaries. This automation has made the distribution process more efficient and transparent.

Furthermore, advancements in privacy technology, such as zero-knowledge proofs, are allowing for more private token distributions. This technology can hide the identity of the sender and receiver in a transaction, making the distribution process more secure and private.

Predictions for the Future of Token Distribution

As we look to the future, we can expect to see more innovation in the token creation and distribution space. We may see more hybrid models of token distribution, combining elements of ICOs, STOs, and DeFi mechanisms.

The use of AI and machine learning could also become prevalent, potentially automating the token distribution process further and making it more efficient. Additionally, we may see more regulatory clarity around token distribution, which could lead to more institutional participation in the space.

Preparing for the Future of Token Creation and Distribution

To prepare for the future of token creation and distribution, it's crucial to stay informed about the latest trends and developments in the space. Regularly reading industry news and participating in blockchain and cryptocurrency communities can help.

Moreover, understanding the legal and regulatory landscape is essential. As regulations evolve, it's crucial to ensure that any token creation or distribution activity complies with the relevant laws and regulations.

Lastly, always consider the technological aspects. Understanding how blockchain technology, smart contracts, and other related technologies work will be increasingly important as these technologies continue to drive innovation in token creation and distribution.

Conclusion

The future of token creation and distribution is exciting and full of possibilities. By staying informed and prepared, you can navigate this evolving landscape effectively. In the next lesson, we will delve into the legal and regulatory considerations in token creation and distribution.

Quiz:

1. What is one emerging trend in token creation and distribution?

2. How are technological advancements impacting token distribution?

3. What is one prediction for the future of token distribution?

4. How can you prepare for the future of token creation and distribution?

4.1: Understanding Economic Models in Tokenomics

Introduction to Economic Models in Tokenomics

Tokenomics, as a discipline, is deeply rooted in economics. The very functionality of tokens, their creation, distribution, and valuation, all revolve around certain economic principles.

These principles, when applied to the world of blockchain and cryptocurrencies, form what we call the Economic Models in Tokenomics.

These models are not just theoretical constructs but are practical frameworks that guide the operation of token-based systems. They help in understanding how value is created and transferred within these systems, how incentives are structured, and how tokens gain and lose value.

The Role of Economic Models in Token-based Systems

Economic models play a pivotal role in shaping the behavior of participants in a token-based system. They help in:

Value Creation: Economic models determine how value is created within a system. This could be through mining, staking, or offering services.

Value Transfer: They also dictate how value is transferred. This could be through transactions, token swaps, or smart contracts.

Incentive Structures: Economic models define the incentive structures that motivate participants to contribute to the system. This could be through rewards, fees, or dividends.

Risk Management: They help manage risks associated with volatility, liquidity, and security.

Regulatory Compliance: Economic models also must consider regulatory compliance, especially when dealing with security tokens.

Overview of Various Economic Models Used in Tokenomics

There are several economic models that have been applied to Tokenomics. Here are a few:

Token Velocity Model: This model shows how quickly tokens are transacted within the system. Higher velocity often means lower token value as tokens don't stay with a holder for long.

Burn-and-Mint Equilibrium Model: This model involves burning (destroying) tokens and minting (creating) new ones to maintain a certain equilibrium in the token supply.

Inflationary and Deflationary Models: These models deal with the increase or decrease in token supply over time. Inflationary models increase token supply, potentially reducing token value. Deflationary models, on the other hand, decrease token supply, potentially increasing token value.

Participation Model: This model rewards participants for their contributions to the network. The more a participant contributes, the more they earn.

Staking Model: In this model, participants 'stake' or lock up their tokens to earn rewards or gain decision-making power in the network.

Each of these models has its own set of advantages and challenges, and the choice of model depends on the specific goals and constraints of the token-based system.

In the subsequent lessons, we will delve deeper into each of these models, explore their workings, and understand their applications in the world of Tokenomics.

Remember, understanding these economic models is key to mastering Tokenomics, as they form the backbone of any token-based system. So, let's dive in and explore these fascinating models!

"Successful investing is about managing risk, not avoiding it."- Benjamin Graham

4.2: Incentive Structures in Token-Based Systems

In this lesson, we will delve into the concept of incentive structures in Tokenomics, the different types of incentive structures used in token-based systems, and their role in promoting network participation and growth.

The Concept of Incentive Structures in Tokenomics

Incentive structures in Tokenomics are mechanisms designed to motivate participants in a blockchain network to contribute and maintain the ecosystem's functionality. These incentives often come in the form of digital tokens, which are awarded based on certain actions or behaviors that align with the network's objectives.

Incentive structures are a fundamental aspect of Tokenomics as they drive network participation, encourage honest behavior, and ensure the long-term sustainability of the blockchain ecosystem. They are often designed in a way that the more a participant contributes to the network, the more they are rewarded.

Types of Incentive Structures Used in Token-Based Systems

There are several types of incentive structures used in token-based systems, each with its own unique characteristics and use cases. Here are a few examples:

Proof of Work (PoW): This is the incentive model used by Bitcoin, where miners are rewarded with tokens for solving complex mathematical problems to validate transactions and add new blocks to the blockchain.

Proof of Stake (PoS): In this model, participants are chosen to confirm transactions, create new blocks based on the number of tokens they hold, and are willing to 'stake' as collateral. The more tokens staked, the higher the chances of being chosen.

Delegated Proof of Stake (DPoS): This model is a PoS variation where token holders vote for a few delegates who will validate transactions and maintain the network. Delegates are incentivized to act honestly, as dishonest behavior could lead to losing their delegate status.

Liquidity Mining: This is a popular incentive structure in Decentralized Finance (DeFi) where users are rewarded with tokens for providing liquidity to a protocol.

The Role of Incentive Structures in Promoting Network Participation and Growth

Incentive structures are crucial in promoting network participation and growth in token-based systems. By rewarding participants with tokens, networks can encourage various beneficial behaviors, such as transaction validation, network security, liquidity provision, and more.

Moreover, these incentive structures can foster a sense of community and mutual benefit among network participants.

As more participants join and contribute to the network, the network grows, becomes more secure, and its tokens potentially increase in value.

This creates a positive feedback loop, where network growth leads to higher token values, which in turn attracts more participants.

In conclusion, understanding incentive structures is crucial for anyone interested in Tokenomics. They are a key component of how token-based systems function, driving participation, ensuring network security, and fostering growth.

In the next lesson, we will explore the concept of token velocity and its role in Tokenomics.

Key Takeaways:

Incentive structures in Tokenomics are designed to motivate participants to contribute to the blockchain network.

There are several types of incentive structures, including Proof of Work, Proof of Stake, Delegated Proof of Stake, and Liquidity Mining.

Incentive structures promote network participation and growth by rewarding beneficial behaviors with tokens.

"Tomorrow's finance is painted in the hues of cryptocurrency, blending the art of technology with the science of economics, crafting a canvas of endless potential."
- Dennis Frank

4.3: Understanding Token Velocity

Lesson Overview

In this lesson, we will delve into one of the key economic concepts in Tokenomics - Token Velocity. We will define what it is, discuss its importance, identify the factors influencing it, and understand its impact on token value and the overall ecosystem.

Definition and Importance of Token Velocity in Tokenomics

Token Velocity refers to the speed at which a digital token is exchanged from one holder to the next within a specific period. It is a measure of how frequently a token is used in transactions within its ecosystem. The concept is akin to the velocity of money in traditional economics, which measures the rate at which money changes hands in an economy.

Token Velocity is a crucial aspect of Tokenomics as it can significantly impact a token's value and the health of the token ecosystem. High token velocity often indicates that tokens are being used frequently for transactions, suggesting a vibrant and active ecosystem.

However, it can also mean that token holders are not incentivized to hold the token for long periods, potentially leading to lower token value.

On the other hand, low velocity may indicate that users are holding onto the token, which could increase its value but also suggest a less active ecosystem.

Factors Influencing Token Velocity

Several factors can influence Token Velocity, including:

1. **Utility and Use Cases:** Tokens with more use cases or utility within their ecosystem tend to have higher velocity as they are used more frequently for transactions.

2. **Incentives for Holding:** If there are incentives for holding a token (like staking rewards or voting rights), users may hold onto their tokens, reducing their velocity.

3. **Transaction Costs:** High transaction costs can discourage frequent transactions, leading to lower token velocity.

4. **Market Sentiment:** In periods of market volatility, token holders may choose to hold or sell their tokens quickly, affecting token velocity.

The Impact of Token Velocity on Token Value and the Overall Ecosystem

Token Velocity can have a significant impact on the value of a token and the health of its ecosystem. A high token velocity can indicate a healthy, active ecosystem with frequent transactions.

However, if tokens are not being held but instead are quickly exchanged, this can put downward pressure on the token's value as supply may exceed demand.

Conversely, low token velocity may suggest that users are holding onto their tokens. This could potentially drive up the token's value as demand exceeds supply.

However, it could also indicate a less active or stagnant ecosystem if tokens are not being used frequently for transactions.

Understanding Token Velocity is, therefore, crucial for anyone involved in the token ecosystem, from token creators to traders and investors. It can provide insights into the token's utility, the behavior of token holders, and the overall health of the token ecosystem.

In the next lesson, we will explore another critical concept in Tokenomics - Token Burn Mechanisms.

Key Takeaways

Token Velocity is a measure of how frequently a token is used in transactions within its ecosystem
.

Several factors influence Token Velocity, including the token's utility, incentives for holding, transaction costs, and market sentiment.

Token Velocity can significantly impact the token's value and the health of the token ecosystem. High velocity can indicate an active ecosystem but may put downward pressure on the token's value. Low velocity may increase the token's value but suggests a less active ecosystem.

"Innovation distinguishes between
a leader and a follower."
- Steve Jobs

4.4: Token Burn Mechanisms and Deflationary Models

Understanding Token Burn Mechanisms

Token burn is a strategy employed by cryptocurrency projects to permanently remove tokens from circulation, effectively reducing the total supply.

This is done by sending a portion of the tokens to an "eater address", a public address from which tokens cannot be spent because the private keys are unobtainable.

This process is known as 'burning' and the tokens are effectively 'burnt' or destroyed. The token burn mechanism is a deflationary measure that can control token supply, stabilize, or increase token price, and incentivize user behavior. It is often used in conjunction with other economic models to optimize the tokenomics of a project.

The Role of Token Burn in Controlling Token Supply

Token burn plays a crucial role in controlling the token supply. By reducing the total number of tokens in circulation, it creates scarcity, which can lead to an increase in the value of the remaining tokens if the demand remains constant or increases.

Token burn can also be used as a tool to combat inflation in token-based ecosystems. By regularly burning tokens, projects can counterbalance the inflationary effects of new token issuance. This can help maintain a balance between supply and demand and stabilize the token price.

Introduction to Deflationary Models in Tokenomics

Deflationary models in Tokenomics are strategies designed to decrease the total supply of tokens over time. Token burn is a common deflationary model, but there are others as well.

For example, some projects implement a deflationary model where a small percentage of each transaction is destroyed or 'burned'. This model, often referred to as 'deflationary yield' or 'rebase', ensures that each token increases in value over time as the total supply decreases.

Deflationary models can be a powerful tool in Tokenomics, creating scarcity and potentially driving up the value of tokens. However, they must be implemented carefully to avoid excessive deflation that could disrupt the token economy.

The Impact of Deflationary Models on Token Value and Market Dynamics

Deflationary models can have a significant impact on token value and market dynamics. By reducing the total supply of tokens, these models can create scarcity, potentially increasing the value of each token.

However, the impact of deflationary models is not always positive. If not effectively managed, they can lead to excessive deflation, which can disrupt the token economy and potentially lead to a decrease in token value.

Furthermore, deflationary models can influence market dynamics by incentivizing certain behaviors. For example, if tokens are burned with each transaction, users might be incentivized to hold their tokens rather than spend them, which could lead to decreased liquidity in the market.

In conclusion, token burn mechanisms and deflationary models are powerful tools in Tokenomics, capable of influencing token supply, value, and market dynamics.

However, they must be used responsibly and strategically to ensure the stability and sustainability of the token economy.

4.5: Network Effects in Tokenomics

Introduction

In this lesson, we will explore the concept of network effects in Tokenomics and how they play a critical role in determining token value and ecosystem growth. We will also discuss strategies that can be used to leverage network effects in token-based systems.

The Concept of Network Effects in Tokenomics

Network effects, a term borrowed from economics and business, refers to the phenomenon where the value or utility of a product or service increases as more people use it.

In the context of Tokenomics, network effects mean that the value of a digital token increases as more people hold it, use it, or participate in its ecosystem.

For instance, consider a cryptocurrency like Bitcoin. The more people who own and use Bitcoin, the more valuable it becomes. This is because increased usage leads to higher demand, and with a capped supply (as is the case with Bitcoin), this can drive up the price.

Furthermore, as more people join the Bitcoin network, it becomes more secure and robust, adding to its intrinsic value.

The Role of Network Effects in Token Value and Ecosystem Growth

Network effects can play a significant role in the growth of a token's ecosystem. As more users join the network, the token's utility can increase, leading to a positive feedback loop. Increased utility can attract more users, which in turn can increase the token's value and utility even further.

For example, Ethereum's network effect is evident in the growth of its ecosystem. As more developers build decentralized applications (dApps) on Ethereum, the utility of Ether (ETH) increases, attracting more users and developers to the network. This network effect has been instrumental in Ethereum's growth and the rise of its native token, Ether.

Strategies to Leverage Network Effects in Token-Based Systems

Leveraging network effects in token-based systems can be a powerful strategy for growth. Here are a few strategies:

1. **Incentivize early adoption:** Early adopters can be rewarded with tokens, which can incentivize them to join the network and contribute to its growth.

2. **Build a strong community:** A strong and engaged community can help drive network effects. This can be achieved through regular communication, transparency, and fostering a sense of ownership among token holders.

3. **Develop partnerships:** Partnerships with other businesses or platforms can help increase the reach of the token and drive network effects.

4. **Ensure token utility:** The token should have a clear utility within its ecosystem. This can drive demand for the token and encourage more users to join the network.

In conclusion, network effects are a crucial aspect of Tokenomics that can significantly influence the value and growth of a token's ecosystem. Understanding and leveraging network effects can be a powerful strategy for anyone involved in the creation or management of digital tokens.

In the next lesson, we will explore case studies of economic models in Tokenomics, where we will see network effects and other economic principles in action.

"Tokenomics is not just an economic model; it's a digital renaissance, painting the future of finance with strokes of code and creativity." – Dennis Frank

4.6: Case Studies of Economic Models in Tokenomics

In this lesson, we will delve into various case studies to understand the practical applications of the economic models in Tokenomics. We will analyze both successful and failed implementations, drawing lessons and insights that can guide us in designing effective economic models for token-based systems.

Analysis of Successful Implementations of Economic Models in Tokenomics

Bitcoin: A Deflationary Model

Bitcoin is the first and most well-known cryptocurrency, and its economic model is a classic example of a deflationary model. Bitcoin has a finite supply of 21 million coins, and the rate at which new bitcoins are created halves approximately every four years in an event known as a "halving". This scarcity and decreasing supply make Bitcoin deflationary, as its value tends to increase over time as demand grows.

Ethereum: Network Effects and Utility

Ethereum's economic model showcases the power of network effects and utility. Ethereum introduced the concept of smart contracts, which greatly expanded the utility of blockchain beyond just a medium of exchange.

This increased utility attracted more users and developers to the Ethereum network, creating a strong network effect. As more people use Ethereum, its network becomes more valuable, and so does its native token, Ether.

Lessons from Failed Implementations

The DAO: A Lesson in Incentive Structures

The Decentralized Autonomous Organization (DAO) was a complex smart contract on the Ethereum blockchain that aimed to create a decentralized venture capital fund.

However, a flaw in its incentive structure led to a catastrophic hack where a third of its funds were siphoned off. This case study highlights the importance of carefully designing incentive structures in token-based systems.

Insights for Designing Effective Economic Models in Token-Based Systems

From these case studies, we can draw several insights:

- **Scarcity and Deflation:** Like Bitcoin, tokens with a finite supply and a decreasing rate of production can create scarcity, which can drive up the token's value if demand increases.

- **Utility and Network Effects:** Like Ethereum, tokens that offer unique utility can attract more users and developers, creating a strong network effect that increases the token's value.

  • **Incentive Structures:** The DAO's failure underscores the importance of designing robust incentive structures. Incentives should align the interests of all participants and protect the system from malicious actors.

In the next lesson, we will explore emerging trends in the economic models in Tokenomics. As the field evolves, new models and strategies are being developed, offering exciting opportunities for innovation in token-based systems.

"The essence of tokenomics lies in the alchemy of technology and economics, transforming bits and bytes into digital gold." - Dennis Frank

4.7: Emerging Trends in Economic Models in Tokenomics

Overview of Emerging Trends in Economic Models in Tokenomics

In the rapidly evolving world of blockchain and cryptocurrencies, the economic models underpinning Tokenomics are also witnessing significant changes. Let's delve into some of the emerging trends that are shaping the future of economic models in Tokenomics.

Decentralized Finance (DeFi)

DeFi is a revolutionary trend that is redefining the economic models in Tokenomics. It refers to the use of blockchain and cryptocurrencies to recreate and improve upon traditional financial systems.

DeFi projects often use unique economic models, such as yield farming and liquidity mining, to incentivize user participation.

Token Burning and Deflationary Models

Deflationary models, particularly token burning, are becoming increasingly popular in Tokenomics. Token burning refers to the process of permanently removing tokens from circulation, which can increase the scarcity and potentially the value of the remaining tokens. This deflationary model is being adopted by various projects to manage token supply and incentivize holding.

Governance Tokens and DAOs

The rise of governance tokens and Decentralized Autonomous Organizations (DAOs) is another noteworthy trend. Governance tokens give holders the right to vote on project decisions, adding a democratic element to the economic model.

DAOs, on the other hand, are organizations run by smart contracts, where token holders can vote on operational decisions.

The Impact of These Trends on the Future of Tokenomics

These emerging trends are not just reshaping the economic models in Tokenomics, but also influencing the future of Tokenomics as a whole.

DeFi is democratizing finance, making it more inclusive and efficient. However, it also brings new challenges such as smart contract vulnerabilities and regulatory uncertainties.

Token burning and deflationary models are adding a new dimension to token valuation. While they can potentially increase token value, they also pose risks such as extreme price volatility.

Governance tokens and DAOs are fostering decentralization and community participation. But they also raise questions about decision-making efficiency and legal accountability.

Preparing for Future Changes in Economic Models in Tokenomics

As we navigate the evolving landscape of Tokenomics, it's crucial to stay informed and adaptable. Here are some ways to prepare for future changes in economic models in Tokenomics:

Continuous Learning: The field of Tokenomics is continuously evolving. Stay updated with the latest trends, research, and discussions in the field.

Risk Management: Understand the risks associated with different economic models. Always do your due diligence before participating in a token-based system.

Regulatory Compliance: Be aware of the regulatory landscape. Compliance with legal requirements is crucial in the ever-changing world of Tokenomics.

In conclusion, the economic models in Tokenomics are undergoing significant changes, driven by trends like DeFi, token burning, and governance tokens.

As we look to the future, continuous learning, risk management, and regulatory compliance will be key to navigating these changes successfully.

"Supply and demand are the scissors of price." - Alfred Marshall

4.8: Review and Future Outlook of Economic Models in Tokenomics

Recap of Key Concepts in Economic Models in Tokenomics

Throughout this module, we have explored various economic models in Tokenomics, each with its unique characteristics and applications. Let's take a moment to recap the key concepts we've covered:

Incentive Structures in Token-Based Systems: Incentive structures are crucial to the success of any token-based system. They motivate participants to contribute to the network, either through mining, staking, or other forms of participation.

Token Velocity: Token velocity refers to the speed at which tokens circulate within the ecosystem. It's a crucial factor in determining the overall health and sustainability of a token economy.

Token Burn Mechanisms and Deflationary Models: Token burn mechanisms are used to reduce the supply of tokens in circulation, creating deflationary pressure. This can increase the value of the remaining tokens, assuming demand remains constant.

Network Effects in Tokenomics: Network effects occur when a network's value increases as more people join or use it. In Tokenomics, network effects can drive the value and utility of a token, encouraging more participation and adoption.

The Future Outlook of Economic Models in Tokenomics

Looking forward, the economic models in Tokenomics will continue to evolve and adapt to the changing landscape of the blockchain and cryptocurrency space. Here are a few trends and predictions:

- **Increased Complexity and Sophistication**: As the field matures, we can expect to see more complex and sophisticated economic models. These models will likely incorporate elements from traditional economics, finance, game theory, and other disciplines.

- **More Experimentation**: The decentralized nature of blockchain technology allows for a high degree of experimentation. This will likely lead to the development of new and innovative economic models.

- **Greater Regulatory Scrutiny**: As token economies become more prevalent, they will likely attract more attention from regulators. This could lead to new regulatory frameworks that impact the design and operation of token economies.

The Role of Economic Models in the Evolution of Tokenomics

Economic models play a critical role in the evolution of Tokenomics. They provide the underlying structure and rules that govern token economies. As such, the development and refinement of these models will be a key factor in the future growth and success of the blockchain and cryptocurrency space.

In conclusion, understanding the economic models in Tokenomics is crucial for anyone involved in the blockchain and cryptocurrency space.

Whether you're a trader, entrepreneur, regulator, or simply a blockchain enthusiast, a solid understanding of these models will give you a deeper insight into the dynamics of token economies and help you make more informed decisions.

In the next module, we will explore the regulatory landscape and compliance issues in Tokenomics.

"In the classroom of tokenomics, every lesson is a key, unlocking the doors to a world where digital currencies dance with economic principles, creating a harmony of knowledge and opportunity."
- Dennis Frank

5.1: Navigating Global Regulatory Frameworks

Introduction

In this lesson, we will delve into the complex world of global regulatory frameworks that govern the issuance and management of digital tokens. As digital tokens transcend national boundaries, understanding these regulations is crucial for anyone involved in the blockchain and cryptocurrency industry.

Global Regulatory Landscape

The regulatory landscape for digital tokens is diverse and complex, with different countries adopting different approaches. Some countries, like Switzerland and Malta, have embraced digital tokens and blockchain technology, creating friendly regulatory environments. Others, like China and India, have imposed strict regulations or outright bans on certain aspects of digital tokens.

United States

In the U.S., the Securities and Exchange Commission (SEC) regulates digital tokens that are considered securities under federal law. The Financial Crimes Enforcement Network (FinCEN) regulates digital tokens under money transmission laws, and the Commodity Futures Trading Commission (CFTC) treats certain digital tokens as commodities.

European Union

In the European Union, digital tokens are regulated under the Markets in Crypto-Assets (MiCA) regulation, which provides legal certainty around crypto-assets not considered as 'financial instruments' under MiFID II and also covers stablecoins.

Asia

In Asia, the regulatory landscape is varied. Japan has been pro-active in regulating digital tokens, with the Financial Services Agency (FSA) providing clear guidelines. South Korea has also enacted regulations to govern digital tokens.

However, in China, Initial Coin Offerings (ICOs) and cryptocurrency exchanges are banned, although the country is actively pursuing blockchain technology.

Regulatory Challenges

Despite the progress made in some jurisdictions, the global regulatory framework for digital tokens is still fragmented and uncertain. This can create challenges for blockchain projects that operate globally. Some of the key challenges include:

Jurisdictional Differences: The regulatory approach to digital tokens varies widely from one jurisdiction to another, creating a complex and often confusing landscape for blockchain projects.

Regulatory Uncertainty: Many jurisdictions have not yet issued specific regulations for digital tokens, leading to uncertainty and risk.

Compliance Costs: Complying with different regulations in different jurisdictions can be costly and time-consuming for blockchain projects.

Conclusion

Navigating the global regulatory frameworks for digital tokens is a complex but necessary task for anyone involved in the blockchain and cryptocurrency industry. As the regulatory landscape continues to evolve, staying informed and adaptable will be key to success.

In the next lesson, we will explore the legal challenges in token issuance and management.

Quiz

Which U.S. regulatory body treats certain digital tokens as commodities?

[ ] Securities and Exchange Commission (SEC)

[ ] Financial Crimes Enforcement Network (FinCEN)

[x] Commodity Futures Trading Commission (CFTC)

[ ] Federal Reserve

What is one of the main challenges in navigating the global regulatory frameworks for digital tokens?

[ ] Lack of technology understanding

[x] Jurisdictional differences

[ ] Too many regulations

[ ] All of the above

In which country are Initial Coin Offerings (ICOs) banned?

[ ] Japan

[ ] South Korea

[x] China

[ ] Switzerland

5.2: Legal Challenges in Token Issuance and Management

The legal landscape of token issuance and management is complex and varies across jurisdictions. This lesson aims to provide an overview of the legal challenges encountered in the token issuance and management process.

We will explore the legal considerations that must be considered when issuing tokens, the regulatory scrutiny that token issuers may face, and the potential legal risks associated with token management.

Legal Considerations in Token Issuance

When issuing tokens, several legal considerations must be considered. These include:

1. **Securities Laws:** Whether a token is classified as a security can have significant legal implications. If a token is classified as a security, it must comply with the relevant securities laws, which can be complex and costly. This includes registration requirements, disclosure obligations, and ongoing reporting requirements.

2. **Consumer Protection Laws:** Token issuers must ensure they do not engage in deceptive or unfair practices. This includes providing accurate and complete information about the token and its associated risks.

3. **Anti-Money Laundering (AML) and Counter-Terrorism Financing (CTF) Laws:** Token issuers must have systems in place to prevent and detect

money laundering and terrorism financing. This includes conducting due diligence on token purchasers and monitoring transactions for suspicious activity.

Regulatory Scrutiny

Regulators worldwide are increasing their scrutiny of token issuances. This can result in regulatory actions, including fines, injunctions, and even criminal charges. Token issuers must be aware of the regulatory environment in which they operate and ensure they comply with all relevant laws and regulations.

Legal Risks in Token Management

Once tokens have been issued, there are several legal risks associated with their management. These include:

Compliance Risks: Token issuers must continue to comply with all relevant laws and regulations. This includes ongoing reporting requirements and maintaining adequate AML and CTF controls.

Contractual Risks: Token issuers must ensure they fulfill all contractual obligations to token holders. This includes delivering any promised goods or services and honoring any rights or benefits associated with the token.

Litigation Risks: Token issuers may face legal action from disgruntled token holders or regulatory authorities. This can result in significant legal costs and reputational damage.

Conclusion

The legal challenges in token issuance and management are significant and should not be underestimated. Token issuers must navigate a complex legal landscape and manage a range of legal risks.

By understanding these challenges and taking proactive steps to address them, token issuers can mitigate their legal risks and increase their chances of success.

In the next lesson, we will delve into Anti-Money Laundering (AML) and Know Your Customer (KYC) compliance in the context of Tokenomics.

"Case studies are the compasses of learning, guiding us through the real-world complexities, illuminating paths of wisdom in uncharted territories." - Dennis Frank

5.3: Anti-Money Laundering and Know Your Customer Compliance

In this lesson, we will delve into two crucial regulatory concepts in the world of Tokenomics: Anti-Money Laundering (AML) and Know Your Customer (KYC) compliance. These regulatory measures are essential in maintaining the integrity of financial systems, including the digital token ecosystems.

Anti-Money Laundering (AML)

Anti-Money Laundering (AML) refers to a set of procedures, laws, and regulations designed to prevent the practice of generating income through illegal actions.

In the context of Tokenomics, AML policies aim to prevent the misuse of digital tokens for illegal purposes such as money laundering or financing terrorism.

AML Compliance in Tokenomics

AML compliance in Tokenomics involves several key components:

Risk Assessment: Identifying and assessing the potential risks of illegal activities associated with a particular token or token transaction.

AML Policies and Procedures: Implementing clear and comprehensive AML policies and procedures to mitigate identified risks.

AML Training: Providing regular training to all relevant personnel on AML policies and procedures.

AML Audits: Conduct regular audits to ensure the effectiveness of AML policies and procedures.

Know Your Customer (KYC)

Know Your Customer (KYC) is a standard in the investment industry that ensures investment advisors know detailed information about their client's risk tolerance, investment knowledge, and financial position.

In the realm of Tokenomics, KYC procedures are used to verify the identity of individuals or entities involved in token transactions.

KYC Compliance in Tokenomics

KYC compliance in Tokenomics involves the following steps:

- **Customer Identification Program (CIP):** Verifying the identity of customers wishing to conduct token transactions.

- **Customer Due Diligence (CDD):** Gathering information about customers to assess their risk profile.

- **Enhanced Due Diligence (EDD):** Conducting more in-depth checks for high-risk customers.

- **Ongoing Monitoring:** Continuously monitoring customer transactions to detect any suspicious activities.

Importance of AML and KYC Compliance in Tokenomics

AML and KYC compliance are critical in Tokenomics for several reasons:

- **Preventing Illegal Activities:** They help prevent illegal activities such as money laundering, terrorist financing, and fraud.

- **Building Trust:** They help build trust among users, investors, and regulators.

- **Regulatory Compliance:** They help token issuers and platforms comply with regulatory requirements, thus avoiding potential fines and penalties.

Conclusion

AML and KYC compliance are integral parts of the regulatory landscape in Tokenomics. By understanding and implementing these measures, token issuers and platforms can ensure the integrity of their operations, build trust with users and investors, and comply with regulatory requirements.

In the next lesson, we will look at some case studies to understand the impact of regulatory measures on Tokenomics.

5.4: Case Studies of Regulatory Impact on Tokenomics

This lesson will delve into several case studies highlighting how regulatory decisions and frameworks have impacted Tokenomics. These case studies will provide real-world examples to understand better the interplay between regulation and the world of digital tokens.

Case Study 1: The DAO and SEC Ruling

The Decentralized Autonomous Organization (DAO) was a digital decentralized venture capital fund that was going to be governed by token holders. However, in 2016, a hacker exploited a vulnerability in the DAO's code and stole a significant amount of Ether.

The incident led to the U.S. Securities and Exchange Commission (SEC) stepping in and declaring that DAO tokens were indeed securities and should have been registered as such.

This ruling significantly impacted the Tokenomics landscape, as it set a precedent for many future ICOs and token offerings, requiring them to comply with securities laws or face severe penalties.

Case Study 2: China's Ban on ICOs

In September 2017, China completely banned ICOs, citing them as disruptive to economic and financial stability. This ban not only halted the creation and trading of digital tokens in one of the world's largest economies, but it also led to a significant drop in global cryptocurrency prices.

This case is an example of how regulatory decisions can have a significant impact on market dynamics and the overall Tokenomics of a region.

Case Study 3: Facebook's Libra

Libra, now known as Diem, is a digital currency project initiated by Facebook. However, the project faced significant regulatory backlash globally due to concerns about potential misuse for money laundering and the threat to monetary sovereignty.

This case study shows how regulatory challenges can hinder even the most ambitious projects, emphasizing the importance of regulatory compliance in Tokenomics.

Case Study 4: Ethereum and the Not-a-Security Declaration

In contrast to the DAO case, the SEC declared in 2018 that Ethereum, despite being initially funded through an ICO, is not a security. The reasoning was that Ethereum had become sufficiently decentralized, with no central party upon which the network depends.

This case study is significant because it shows that the regulatory classification of tokens can be fluid and may change as the project evolves.

Conclusion

These case studies highlight the profound impact that regulatory decisions can have on Tokenomics. They underscore the importance of understanding and complying with relevant regulations when creating, distributing, or trading digital tokens.

6.1: Understanding Case Studies in Tokenomics

Introduction to the Importance of Case Studies in Understanding Tokenomics

Case studies play a crucial role in studying and understanding any subject, and Tokenomics is no exception. They provide a practical perspective on theoretical concepts, allowing us to see how these concepts are applied in real-world situations.

By examining the successes and failures of various token projects, we can gain valuable insights into the dynamics of Tokenomics.

In the context of Tokenomics, case studies can help us understand how different types of tokens function, how they are valued, how they are distributed, and how they interact with various economic models. They also shed light on the regulatory challenges token projects face and how they can be navigated.

How to Analyze Case Studies for Insights and Lessons

When analyzing case studies in Tokenomics, it is important to approach them systematically. Here are some steps to guide you:

1. **Understand the Context:** Begin by understanding the background of the token project. What problem is it trying to solve? What is its target market? What is its unique selling proposition?

2. **Examine the Token Model:** Look at the type of token used, its utility, and its distribution mechanism. How does the token facilitate transactions within its ecosystem? How is it incentivizing users?

3. **Evaluate the Economic Model:** Analyze the economic model used by the token. How does it ensure the token's value? How does it manage supply and demand?

4. **Consider the Regulatory Landscape:** Consider the regulatory challenges faced by the project. How did it comply with legal requirements? Were there any legal issues that impacted its success?

5. **Assess the Outcome:** Finally, assess the outcome of the project. Was it successful? If not, why did it fail? What lessons can be learned from its failure?

Discussion on the Role of Real-World Applications in Shaping Tokenomics

Real-world applications have a significant impact on shaping Tokenomics. They provide practical proof of how Tokenomics can be used to facilitate transactions, incentivize users, and create value within a blockchain ecosystem.

For instance, the rise of Decentralized Finance (DeFi) applications has led to the creation of various types of tokens, each with its unique economic model. These applications have not only demonstrated the potential of Tokenomics but have also highlighted its challenges, particularly in terms of regulatory compliance.

By studying these real-world applications, we can gain a better understanding of the practical aspects of Tokenomics, which can help us develop more effective and efficient token models in the future.

In conclusion, case studies and real-world applications are invaluable resources in the study of Tokenomics. They provide us with practical insights and lessons that can help us understand the dynamics of Tokenomics and guide us in the creation and management of successful token projects.

Markets can remain irrational longer than you can remain solvent." - John Maynard Keynes

6.2: Success Stories in Tokenomics

In this lesson, we will delve into some of the most successful token projects and analyze the strategies that led to their triumph. By understanding these success stories, we can glean valuable insights and lessons that can be applied to future token projects.

Analysis of Successful Token Projects and Their Strategies

Bitcoin (BTC)

As the pioneer of cryptocurrencies, Bitcoin's success story is nothing short of legendary. Bitcoin's tokenomics is based on a deflationary model, with a maximum supply of 21 million coins. This scarcity, combined with its first-mover advantage, has contributed to its high value and widespread adoption.

Ethereum (ETH)

Ethereum introduced the concept of smart contracts and paved the way for the tokenization of digital assets. Its token, Ether, is a cryptocurrency and a utility token used to pay for transaction fees and computational services on the Ethereum network. This dual functionality has been a key factor in Ethereum's success.

Binance Coin (BNB)

Binance Coin started as an ERC-20 token before migrating to its own blockchain, Binance Chain. BNB's success can be attributed to its utility within the Binance ecosystem, where it can be used for trading fee discounts, participation in token sales, and more. Binance also employs a token burn mechanism, which helps maintain BNB's value.

Understanding the Factors That Contributed to Their Success

While each of these tokens has its unique factors contributing to their success, there are some common themes:

Utility and Functionality: Each of these tokens serves a specific purpose within their respective ecosystems, whether it's paying for transactions, participating in network governance, or getting trading fee discounts.

Scarcity and Deflationary Mechanisms: Bitcoin and Binance Coin have implemented scarcity and deflationary mechanisms, respectively, which help maintain and increase their value over time.

Community and Network Effects: All three tokens have strong communities and network effects, which increase their value as more people use and hold them.

Lessons Learned from These Success Stories

Here are some key takeaways from these success stories:

- **Utility is Key:** Tokens that serve a specific purpose within their ecosystem tend to be more successful.

- **Scarcity Matters:** Tokens with a limited supply or deflationary mechanisms can help maintain and increase their value.

- **Community is Crucial**: A strong community can drive a token's adoption and increase its network effects.

In conclusion, understanding the tokenomics behind successful projects can provide valuable insights for future token projects.

However, it's important to remember that what worked for one project may not necessarily work for another, as success in tokenomics depends on a variety of factors, including the project's unique value proposition, market conditions, and regulatory environment.

"Learning tokenomics is a journey, turning each concept into a steppingstone towards mastering the dance of digital finance."
- Dennis Frank

6.3: Lessons from Failed Token Projects

In this lesson, we will examine several token projects that did not succeed. We will analyze the reasons for their failures and derive key takeaways and lessons from these experiences. This analysis will provide valuable insights that can help in avoiding similar pitfalls in future token projects.

Examination of Token Projects That Did Not Succeed

Let's start by examining some token projects that did not meet their objectives. Some of these projects include:

The DAO: The DAO was a decentralized autonomous organization that raised over $150 million in its ICO in 2016. However, it was hacked due to a vulnerability in its smart contract, leading to a loss of around $50 million.

Tezos: Tezos raised $232 million in its ICO in 2017. However, it faced numerous legal challenges and internal conflicts that delayed the project and eroded investor confidence.

BitConnect: BitConnect was a high-yield cryptocurrency investment Ponzi scheme that collapsed in 2018, leading to investor losses of over $1 billion.

Analysis of the Reasons for Their Failure

The reasons for the failure of these projects varied, but some common themes emerged:

Poor Security: In the case of the DAO, the failure was due to a security vulnerability in the smart contract. This highlights the importance of rigorous security audits and testing in token projects.

Legal and Regulatory Challenges: Tezos faced numerous legal and regulatory challenges, highlighting the importance of understanding, and navigating the complex regulatory landscape for token projects.

Fraudulent Practices: BitConnect was a Ponzi scheme that promised high returns to investors. This underscores the importance of transparency and ethical practices in token projects.

Key Takeaways and Lessons from These Failures

From these failures, we can derive some key lessons

- **Security is paramount:** Token projects must prioritize security to protect investor funds and maintain trust in the project.

- **Regulatory compliance is crucial:** Token projects must understand and navigate the complex regulatory landscape to avoid legal challenges that can derail the project.

- **Transparency and ethics are key:** Token projects must operate with transparency and adhere to ethical practices to maintain investor trust and avoid fraudulent practices.

In conclusion, while the failure of these token projects was unfortunate, they provide valuable lessons for future token projects. By learning from these failures, we can avoid similar pitfalls and increase the chances of success in future token projects.

6.4: Case Study: Bitcoin and its Impact on Tokenomics

Overview of Bitcoin's Token Model

Bitcoin, the first and most well-known cryptocurrency, is a prime example of Tokenomics in action. The Bitcoin network operates on a peer-to-peer system where transactions are verified by network nodes through cryptography and recorded on a public ledger called a blockchain.

Bitcoin's token model is based on Proof of Work (PoW) consensus mechanism and is deflationary in nature. The total supply of Bitcoin is capped at 21 million, and the rate of new Bitcoin creation halves approximately every four years in an event known as the "halving." This scarcity is a key feature of Bitcoin's economic model and is a major factor in its price dynamics.

Analysis of Bitcoin's Impact on the Tokenomics Landscape

Bitcoin's innovative token model has had a profound impact on the Tokenomics landscape. It introduced the world to the concept of decentralized digital money and demonstrated that a network could maintain consensus without central authority.

The success of Bitcoin has spurred the creation of thousands of other cryptocurrencies, each with their own unique token model. Bitcoin's influence can be seen in many of these models, particularly those that also use a PoW consensus mechanism or a deflationary model.

Bitcoin also introduced the concept of initial coin offerings (ICOs), a method of crowdfunding that has been used by many projects to raise capital. ICOs have become a significant part of the Tokenomics landscape, despite the regulatory challenges they face.

Lessons Learned from Bitcoin's Market Dynamics

Bitcoin's market dynamics offer several valuable lessons. The first is the importance of scarcity in a token model. Bitcoin's price has risen dramatically over the years, in large part due to its capped supply and increasing demand.

Another lesson is the impact of market sentiment and speculation on token prices. Bitcoin's price has experienced significant volatility, driven in large part by speculative trading. This highlights the need for traders and investors to understand the underlying token model and market dynamics.

Finally, Bitcoin's success underscores the potential of decentralized systems. Despite numerous challenges, including regulatory scrutiny and technical issues, Bitcoin has demonstrated the viability of decentralized, blockchain-based financial systems.

In conclusion, Bitcoin's token model and its impact on the Tokenomics landscape provide valuable insights for anyone interested in the economics of cryptocurrencies. Its success and challenges offer important lessons for future token models and highlight the dynamic and evolving nature of Tokenomics.

"Beware of little expenses. A small leak will sink a great ship."
- Benjamin Franklin

6.5: Case Study: Ethereum and the Rise of Smart Contracts

Understanding Ethereum's Token Model and the Role of Smart Contracts

Ethereum, launched in 2015, is a blockchain-based platform that introduced the concept of "smart contracts". Smart contracts are self-executing contracts with the terms of the agreement directly written into code.

They automatically execute transactions when predefined conditions are met, eliminating the need for a middleman.
Ethereum's native token, Ether (ETH), serves two primary purposes. First, it is a digital currency just like Bitcoin that can be sent and received.

Second, and more importantly, it is used to pay for transaction fees and computational services on the Ethereum network. This dual functionality of Ether is a perfect example of the utility token in Tokenomics.

Analysis of Ethereum's Contribution to the Tokenomics Ecosystem

Ethereum's introduction of smart contracts has revolutionized the blockchain and Tokenomics ecosystem. It has enabled the development of Decentralized Applications (DApps) and made it possible for developers to create their own tokens on the Ethereum platform using the ERC-20 token standard.

ERC-20 has emerged as the technical standard used for all smart contracts on the Ethereum blockchain for token implementation. A large majority of tokens in the crypto ecosystem are ERC-20 tokens. This has significantly contributed to the growth and diversity of tokens in the market, expanding the scope of Tokenomics.

Insights Gained from Ethereum's Market Performance

Ethereum's market performance provides valuable insights into the dynamics of Tokenomics. Despite being second to Bitcoin in market capitalization, Ethereum's impact on the blockchain ecosystem has been profound due to its smart contract functionality.

Ether's price is influenced by factors such as demand for DApps, the number of transactions on the network, and the overall activity on the Ethereum platform. This case highlights the fact that a token's value is not only determined by its role as a medium of exchange but also its utility within its respective ecosystem.

Ethereum's transition from Proof of Work (PoW) to Proof of Stake (PoS) consensus mechanism, known as Ethereum 2.0, also has significant implications for Tokenomics. This transition is expected to reduce transaction fees and increase transaction speed, potentially leading to an increase in Ether's value.

Conclusion

Ethereum's innovative approach to Tokenomics, with the introduction of smart contracts and the ERC-20 token standard, has had a transformative impact on the blockchain ecosystem.

The case of Ethereum highlights the importance of utility in determining a token's value and the role of Tokenomics in shaping the functionality and success of a blockchain platform. As Ethereum continues to evolve, it provides a wealth of insights for understanding the future trends in Tokenomics.

6.6: Case Study: DeFi Tokens and Yield Farming

Examination of DeFi tokens and the concept of yield farming

Decentralized Finance (DeFi) has emerged as a transformative force in the blockchain ecosystem. At the heart of this revolution are DeFi tokens, which play a crucial role in the functioning and governance of DeFi protocols.

Yield farming, also known as liquidity mining, is a popular strategy used by DeFi users to maximize returns by leveraging different DeFi tokens.

Yield farming involves lending or staking DeFi tokens in a liquidity pool, which is a smart contract that holds funds.

In return for their service, liquidity providers are rewarded with fees and yield farming tokens. This process creates a high-yield, albeit risky, opportunity for token holders to earn passive income.

Analysis of the economic models behind DeFi tokens

The economic models behind DeFi tokens vary by protocol, but they generally revolve around incentivizing user participation and maintaining protocol stability. Here are some common economic models:

Inflationary model: New tokens are minted as rewards for liquidity providers. This encourages participation but can lead to token price depreciation if not managed properly.

Deflationary model: Some protocols burn a portion of the transaction fees, reducing the token supply over time and potentially increasing the token's price.

Staking model: Users can stake their tokens to participate in the protocol's governance and earn staking rewards.

Fee model: Transaction fees are distributed to token holders, creating a direct revenue stream for participants.

Lessons learned from the rise and challenges of DeFi tokens

The rise of DeFi tokens and yield farming has brought valuable lessons to the blockchain industry:

Risk and reward: Yield farming can offer high returns, but it also comes with significant risks, including smart contract bugs, market volatility, and impermanent loss. Users must thoroughly understand these risks before participating.

Importance of governance: Token-based governance has become a standard in DeFi protocols. However, it is crucial to ensure fair token distribution to avoid centralization of voting power.

Regulatory challenges: The regulatory landscape for DeFi tokens is still uncertain. Protocols must be prepared to adapt to potential regulatory changes.

Scalability issues: The rapid growth of DeFi has led to scalability issues on networks like Ethereum, leading to high transaction fees. This highlights the need for more scalable blockchain solutions.

In conclusion, DeFi tokens and yield farming represent a significant advancement in the blockchain and Tokenomics field. They offer new ways for users to earn returns and participate in protocol governance.

However, they also bring new challenges and risks that must be carefully managed. As the DeFi sector continues to evolve, it will be interesting to see how these Tokenomics models adapt and mature.

6.7: Case Study: NFTs and the Tokenization of Digital Assets

Understanding the Token Model Behind NFTs

Non-Fungible Tokens (NFTs) have emerged as a novel category of digital assets in the blockchain ecosystem. Unlike fungible tokens such as Bitcoin or Ethereum, where each token is identical and interchangeable, NFTs are unique and distinguishable from each other. This uniqueness is the core characteristic that gives NFTs their value and use case.

NFTs are typically built on the Ethereum blockchain, leveraging the ERC-721 token standard. This standard ensures that each token has a unique identifier and metadata associated with it, which can include attributes like owner, history of ownership, and any other relevant information.

The uniqueness and the ability to verify ownership make NFTs a perfect solution for tokenizing digital assets like art, music, virtual real estate, and more. This has opened up new possibilities for artists and creators to monetize their work in ways that were not possible before.

Analysis of the Market Dynamics and Valuation of NFTs

The NFT market has seen explosive growth in recent times. A combination of factors, including the rise of digital art, increased interest in cryptocurrencies, and the desire for digital ownership in the virtual world, has driven this boom.

Valuation of NFTs is a complex process and is often subjective. Unlike fungible tokens, which have a clear market price, the value of an NFT is largely determined by what someone is willing to pay for it. This can be influenced by factors such as the reputation of the creator, rarity of the asset, and the demand in the market.

However, it is important to note that the NFT market is highly volatile and speculative. Prices can fluctuate wildly, and there is a risk of a market bubble, similar to what has been observed in other areas of the cryptocurrency market.

Insights and Lessons from the NFT Boom

The NFT boom has provided several key insights and lessons. Firstly, it has demonstrated the potential of blockchain technology to disrupt traditional industries, in this case, the art and music industry.

Artists and creators can now directly monetize their work without intermediaries, and buyers can verify the authenticity and ownership of digital assets.

Secondly, it has highlighted the speculative nature of the crypto market. The high prices paid for some NFTs have raised concerns about a potential market bubble and the sustainability of these prices in the long term.

Finally, the NFT boom has brought attention to the environmental impact of blockchain technology. The process of minting NFTs is energy-intensive and contributes to the carbon footprint of the blockchain industry. This has sparked discussions about the need for more sustainable blockchain solutions.

In conclusion, the rise of NFTs and the tokenization of digital assets is a fascinating case study in the field of Tokenomics. It provides valuable insights into the potential of blockchain technology, the dynamics of the crypto market, and the challenges that need to be addressed for sustainable growth.

It also sets the stage for the future of Tokenomics, as we continue to explore new ways to tokenize and monetize digital assets.

6.8: Future Trends in Tokenomics from Past Case Studies

In this lesson, we will forecast future trends in Tokenomics by analyzing past case studies. We will discuss the potential impact of these trends on the Tokenomics landscape and prepare lessons for traders, entrepreneurs, and regulators.

Forecasting Future Trends Based on Past Case Studies

The best way to predict the future is to understand the past. By studying the successes and failures of past token projects, we can identify patterns and trends that may shape the future of Tokenomics.

For instance, the rise of Bitcoin demonstrated the potential of decentralized digital currencies, leading to the creation of thousands of alternative cryptocurrencies. Ethereum's success highlighted the potential of smart contracts and led to the explosion of decentralized applications (dApps) and DeFi projects.

On the other hand, the failure of many ICOs due to a lack of transparency and regulatory compliance has led to a shift toward more regulated token issuance mechanisms like STOs and IEOs.

Potential Impact of Future Trends on the Tokenomics Landscape

The future trends in Tokenomics will undoubtedly significantly impact the landscape of digital tokens. The rise of DeFi and yield farming has already started to reshape the Tokenomics landscape, with DeFi tokens and governance tokens becoming increasingly popular. The growing interest in NFTs is leading to new token models and use cases for digital tokens.

Moreover, the increasing regulatory scrutiny and the push for more transparency and accountability in token projects are likely to lead to more robust and compliant Tokenomics models.

Preparing for the Future: Lessons for Traders, Entrepreneurs, and Regulators

As we look toward the future, there are several lessons that traders, entrepreneurs, and regulators can learn from past case studies.

Traders: The volatility and unpredictability of the token market make it essential for traders to understand the underlying Tokenomics of the tokens they trade. By understanding the token supply mechanisms, utility, and economic models, traders can make more informed investment decisions.

Entrepreneurs: For entrepreneurs planning to launch their own tokens, understanding the successes and failures of past token projects can provide invaluable insights. They can learn from the mistakes of failed projects and emulate the strategies of successful ones. Moreover, understanding the regulatory landscape and compliance requirements is crucial to avoid legal issues.

Regulators: For regulators, past case studies can provide insights into the challenges and risks associated with digital tokens. They can use these insights to develop more effective regulatory frameworks that protect investors without stifling innovation.

In conclusion, by studying past case studies, we can forecast future trends in Tokenomics, understand their potential impact, and prepare for the future.

As we move forward, it is crucial for all stakeholders to understand and adapt to these trends to navigate the ever-evolving Tokenomics landscape successfully.

"In the short run, the market is a voting machine but in the long run, it is a weighing machine."
-Benjamin Graham

6.9: Review and Analysis of Real-World Applications

In this lesson, we will review and analyze real-world applications of Tokenomics across various industries. We will delve into the impact and effectiveness of these applications, and discuss the lessons learned and future implications for these sectors.

Real-World Applications of Tokenomics Across Various Industries

Tokenomics is not just a theoretical concept; it has practical applications across a wide range of industries. Here are a few examples:

- **Finance:** In the financial sector, Tokenomics has been instrumental in the rise of Decentralized Finance (DeFi) applications. Tokens are used as a medium of exchange, a store of value, and a unit of account in these systems. They also play a crucial role in governance, allowing token holders to vote on system upgrades and changes.

- **Gaming:** In the gaming industry, Tokenomics is used to create in-game assets in the form of Non-Fungible Tokens (NFTs). These assets can be traded on blockchain platforms, creating a new economy within the gaming ecosystem.

- **Real Estate:** Tokenomics is also finding its way into the real estate sector. Property ownership can be tokenized, allowing for fractional ownership and easier transfer of assets.

- **Supply Chain:** In supply chain management, Tokenomics can be used to track and trace goods, ensuring transparency and accountability.

127

Analysis of the Impact and Effectiveness of These Applications

The impact and effectiveness of Tokenomics in these industries have been significant:

- In the **financial sector**, DeFi applications have democratized access to financial services, allowing anyone with an internet connection to participate in global finance.

- In the **gaming industry**, NFTs have created new revenue streams for developers and given players ownership of their in-game assets.

- In the **real estate sector**, tokenization has made property investment more accessible and liquid.

- In the **supply chain industry**, Tokenomics has improved transparency and accountability, reducing fraud and counterfeiting.

Lessons Learned and Future Implications

The real-world applications of Tokenomics have provided valuable lessons:

- **Interoperability is key:** For tokens to be effective, they must be interoperable with other systems. This requires standardization and collaboration among different blockchain platforms.

- **Regulation is a double-edged sword:** While regulation can provide legitimacy and protection for token users, it can also stifle innovation if not implemented carefully.

- **User experience matters:** For Tokenomics to gain widespread adoption, it must be user-friendly. This means creating intuitive interfaces and educating users about the benefits and risks of tokens.

Looking forward, the applications of Tokenomics are expected to expand as more industries recognize its potential. However, challenges remain, including regulatory uncertainty, technical complexity, and the need for more robust security measures.

By learning from past applications and anticipating future trends, we can navigate these challenges and unlock the full potential of Tokenomics.
In the next lesson, we will delve into a detailed analysis and discussion of various case studies in Tokenomics.

"The four most dangerous words in investing are: 'this time it's different.'" - Sir John Templeton

6.10: Case Study Analysis and Discussion

Welcome to the final lesson of Module 6, where we will be analyzing and discussing the case studies we have learned about so far. This lesson is designed to be interactive, encouraging you to engage in critical thinking exercises and draw insights from the case studies.

Interactive Session: Analyzing Case Studies

We have studied a variety of case studies in this module, each presenting unique insights into the application of tokenomics in the real world. Let's revisit these case studies and delve deeper into the key aspects of each.

Bitcoin and its Impact on Tokenomics

Bitcoin, as the first cryptocurrency, has had a significant impact on the field of tokenomics. Consider the following questions:

- What were the key economic principles that Bitcoin introduced?

- How did Bitcoin's tokenomics influence its adoption and growth?

- What challenges did Bitcoin face due to its tokenomics?

Ethereum and the Rise of Smart Contracts

Ethereum brought a new dimension to tokenomics with the introduction of smart contracts. Reflect on these points:

1. How did smart contracts revolutionize tokenomics?

2. What role did Ethereum's tokenomics play in fostering a vibrant ecosystem of decentralized applications (dApps)?

3. What challenges did Ethereum face due to its tokenomics?

DeFi Tokens and Yield Farming

DeFi tokens and yield farming have become prominent aspects of the blockchain landscape. Consider these points:

- How have DeFi tokens changed the tokenomics landscape?

- What role does yield farming play in the tokenomics of DeFi projects?

- What are some of the risks and challenges associated with the tokenomics of DeFi tokens and yield farming?

NFTs and the Tokenization of Digital Assets

NFTs have opened new possibilities for tokenization. Reflect on these questions:

- How has the tokenomics of NFTs influenced their adoption and use? What are the unique aspects of NFT tokenomics compared to other types of tokens? What are some of the challenges and risks associated with the tokenomics of NFTs?

Critical Thinking Exercises

Now that we have revisited these case studies, it is time for you to apply your knowledge. Consider the following:

1. How do the tokenomics of these different projects compare?

2. What lessons can be learned from the successes and failures of these projects? • How might these lessons apply to future token projects?

Wrap-Up and Key Takeaways

This module has provided a comprehensive overview of real-world applications of tokenomics. We have explored a range of case studies, each offering unique insights into how tokenomics can drive the success or failure of a project.

Here are some key takeaways:

- Tokenomics plays a crucial role in the success or failure of a blockchain project.

- Different types of tokens, such as Bitcoin, Ethereum, DeFi tokens, and NFTs, each have unique tokenomics that influence their functionality and use. Understanding the tokenomics of a project can provide valuable insights into its potential risks and rewards.

In the next module, we will delve into the market dynamics and token valuation. We look forward to seeing you there!

"Tokenomics: The heartbeat of blockchain projects, where each token beats to its own rhythm, shaping success, functionality, and the balance of risk and reward."
- Dennis Frank

7.1: Understanding Market Sentiment in Tokenomics

Introduction to Market Sentiment and Its Role in Token Valuation

Market sentiment, also known as investor sentiment, refers to the overall attitude of investors toward a particular security or financial market. In the context of Tokenomics, market sentiment plays a crucial role in the valuation of digital tokens.

It is the collective feeling or mood of token holders and potential investors about the future of a token. This sentiment can significantly influence the demand for a token and consequently, its price.

Gauging Market Sentiment in the Crypto Space

In the crypto space, gauging market sentiment can be a bit complex due to the volatility and speculative nature of the market. However, several tools and indicators can help understand the mood of the market. These include:

- **Price Trends**: A token's price trend can provide insights into market sentiment. If prices are consistently rising, the market sentiment is likely bullish. Conversely, falling prices may indicate bearish sentiment.

- **Trading Volume**: High trading volumes often suggest strong investor interest and positive market sentiment. On the other hand, low volumes may indicate a lack of interest or negative sentiment.

- **Social Media and Online Forums**: Platforms like Twitter, Reddit, and various cryptocurrency forums are often used by crypto enthusiasts to express their views and predictions about different tokens. Analyzing these discussions can provide valuable insights into market sentiment.

The Impact of Market Sentiment on Token Prices

Market sentiment can significantly impact token prices. Positive sentiment can lead to increased demand for a token, pushing its price up. Conversely, negative sentiment can result in selling pressure, leading to a price drop.

It is important to note that market sentiment can sometimes lead to extreme price movements, resulting in market bubbles or crashes.

The Role of News, Social Media, and Influencers in Shaping Market Sentiment

News events, social media discussions, and influencers play a significant role in shaping market sentiment in the crypto space. Positive news or endorsements from influential figures can lead to increased investor confidence, driving up token prices.

On the other hand, negative news or critical comments from influencers can trigger panic selling, leading to price drops. For instance, Elon Musk's tweets have been known to cause significant price movements in the crypto market. His endorsement of Dogecoin on Twitter led to a massive price surge, while his announcement that Tesla would no longer accept Bitcoin as payment caused a significant price drop.

Case Studies Illustrating the Influence of Market Sentiment on Token Valuation

Let's look at a couple of case studies to illustrate the influence of market sentiment on token valuation:

Case Study 1: Bitcoin's 2017 Bull Run

In 2017, Bitcoin experienced a massive bull run, with its price reaching nearly $20,000. This price surge was largely driven by positive market sentiment, fueled by widespread media coverage and growing interest from institutional investors.

Case Study 2: The Impact of China's Crypto Ban

In 2021, China announced a crackdown on crypto mining and trading, leading to a significant drop in Bitcoin's price. This negative news event led to a shift in market sentiment from bullish to bearish, resulting in a market-wide sell-off.

These case studies highlight the significant impact that market sentiment can have on token valuation. As such, understanding market sentiment is crucial for anyone involved in the crypto space, whether you're a trader, investor, or token issuer.

"Envisioning a virtual economy, where business professionals see a future of finance illuminated by the innovative glow of Bitcoin and cryptocurrency."
- Dennis Frank

7.2: Factors Influencing Token Pricing

Introduction

In this lesson, we will delve into a range of factors that influence token pricing. Understanding these factors is crucial for anyone involved in the cryptocurrency market, whether you're a trader, an investor, or a blockchain enthusiast. By the end of this lesson, you should be able to comprehend the dynamics that drive the prices of tokens in the market.

The Role of Supply and Demand in Token Pricing

Like any other market, the price of tokens is primarily determined by supply and demand. The basic economic principle holds that the price tends to rise when the demand for a token exceeds its supply. Conversely, if the supply of a token surpasses the demand, the price is likely to fall.

For instance, when a token is listed on a major exchange, it often increases demand, which can drive up the price. Similarly, a large-scale sell-off by token holders can increase the supply in the market, leading to a decrease in price.

How Token Utility and Functionality Impact its Price

The utility and functionality of a token play a significant role in its pricing. Tokens that offer unique features or services, or those that are integral to the functioning of a particular blockchain ecosystem, tend to have higher demand, which can positively impact their price.

For example, Ethereum's Ether (ETH) is used to pay for transaction fees and computational services on the Ethereum network, making it highly functional and valuable within its ecosystem.

This utility contributes to its market demand and, consequently, its price.

The Influence of Macroeconomic Factors on Token Pricing

Macroeconomic factors such as inflation rates, interest rates, and economic growth can also influence token prices. For instance, during times of economic instability or inflation, investors may turn to cryptocurrencies as a hedge against traditional financial systems, driving up demand and prices.

Moreover, global events such as political unrest, regulatory changes, or technological advancements can also impact the cryptocurrency market and token prices.

Understanding Market Manipulation and its Effect on Token Prices

Market manipulation is another factor that can significantly influence token prices. This can occur in various forms, such as 'pump and dump' schemes, where the price of a token is artificially inflated to attract investors and then sold off in large quantities, causing the price to plummet.

While most reputable exchanges have measures in place to prevent such practices, market manipulation is still a risk in the largely unregulated cryptocurrency market, and it's crucial for investors to be aware of this. The Impact of Regulatory News and Events on

Token Pricing

Regulatory news and events can have a significant impact on token prices. Positive regulatory news, such as a country legalizing cryptocurrency or a major financial institution adopting blockchain technology, can lead to an increase in token prices.

On the other hand, negative news, such as regulatory crackdowns on cryptocurrencies or major hacks, can lead to a decrease in token prices. Therefore, staying updated with the latest regulatory news and events is crucial for anyone involved in the cryptocurrency market.

Conclusion

In conclusion, the pricing of tokens in the cryptocurrency market is influenced by a multitude of factors, including supply and demand, token utility and functionality, macroeconomic factors, market manipulation, and regulatory news and events.

Understanding these factors can provide valuable insights into market dynamics and help make informed decisions in the cryptocurrency market.

In the next lesson, we will delve deeper into token valuation models, which provide a more systemic approach to understanding token prices.

"The goal of a successful trader is to make the best trades. Money is secondary." - Alexander Elder

7.3: Introduction to Token Valuation Models

Understanding the Concept of Token Valuation

Token valuation is a fundamental concept in Tokenomics that refers to determining a digital token's intrinsic value. This value is derived from various factors such as the token's utility, demand, supply, and the overall health of the token's ecosystem.

It's important to note that token valuation is not about predicting short-term price movements, but rather about understanding the fundamental worth of a token.

The Difference Between Token Price and Token Value

Before we delve into token valuation models, it's crucial to distinguish between a token's price and its value. The **price** of a token is what you pay to acquire it in the market. It's determined by supply and demand dynamics and can be influenced by various factors such as market sentiment, news events, and market manipulation.

On the other hand, the **value** of a token is its intrinsic worth, which is derived from its utility, the strength of its ecosystem, and its potential for future growth. The value of a token is what you get, and ideally, you want to buy tokens whose price is lower than their value.

Overview of Various Token Valuation Models

There are several models used to value tokens. Here's an overview of some of the most common ones:

1. **Discounted Cash Flow (DCF) Model**: This model is often used for security tokens that represent an

underlying cash-generating asset. It involves estimating the future cash flows that the token will generate and then discounting them back to their present value.

2. **Network Value to Transactions (NVT) Ratio**: This model is akin to the Price-to-Earnings ratio in traditional finance. It involves comparing the network value (market cap) of a token to the volume of transactions on its network.

3. **Metcalfe's Law**: This model values tokens based on the size of their network. It's based on the premise that the value of a network is proportional to the square of the number of its users.

4. **Burniske's Equation of Exchange Model**: This model values utility tokens based on their velocity and the economic activity of their network.

Each of these models has its strengths and limitations, and they are often used in combination to arrive at a more comprehensive valuation.

The Role of Tokenomics in Token Valuation

Tokenomics plays a crucial role in token valuation. The design of a token's economic system can significantly influence its value.

For instance, a token with a well-designed incentive structure that encourages users to hold and use the token can increase demand and, thus, its value. On the other hand, a token with a high inflation rate can dilute its value.

In conclusion, token valuation is a complex process that requires a deep understanding of Tokenomics. In the following lessons, we will delve deeper into each of these valuation models and learn how to apply them in practice.

In the next lesson, we will delve into an in-depth analysis of token valuation models.

"In the tapestry of tomorrow's finance, each thread of cryptocurrency weaves a pattern of innovation and adaptation, beckoning a future rich with possibility."
- Dennis Frank

7.4: In-depth Analysis of Token Valuation Models

In this lesson, we will delve into the various token valuation models used in the cryptocurrency market. Understanding these models will provide you with the tools to assess the underlying value of different tokens, which can be a critical factor in making informed investment decisions.

Cost of Production Model

The cost of production model is a valuation model that considers the cost of producing a token or cryptocurrency. This model is often applied to cryptocurrencies like Bitcoin, where mining is a significant part of the token creation process.

The cost of production model considers factors such as:

- The cost of the hardware used for mining

- The electricity cost involved in mining

- The mining Reward

By understanding these costs, you can estimate the minimum value of a token, below which it would not be profitable for miners to continue producing the token.

Network Value to Transactions (NVT) Ratio Model

The NVT ratio model is a valuation model that compares the value of a token's network to the volume of transactions on the network. It is like the Price/Earnings (P/E) ratio used in traditional finance.

The NVT ratio is calculated as:

[NVT Ratio = Network Volume / Transaction Volume]

A high NVT ratio may suggest that the network is overvalued compared to the volume of transactions it is processing. Conversely, a low NVT ratio may suggest that the network is undervalued.

Equation of Exchange Model (MV=PQ)

The equation of exchange model is a monetary economics model that can be adapted for token valuation. The model is expressed as MV=PQ, where:

- M is the total supply of money (or in this case, tokens)

- V is the velocity of money (how frequently tokens are used in transactions)

- P is the price level

- Q is the index of real expenditures (the volume of transactions)

This model can be used to estimate a token's value based on its use in transactions.

Discounted Cash Flow (DCF) Model

The discounted cash flow (DCF) model is a valuation model used in traditional finance that can also be adapted for token valuation. This model involves estimating the future cash flows that a token will generate and then discounting those cash flows back to their present value.

In the context of token valuation, "cash flows" could be interpreted as the benefits received from holding or using a token. For example, a token might provide holders with a share of transaction fees, voting rights, or other benefits.

Case Studies

To illustrate the application of these valuation models, we will look at several case studies:

- Bitcoin: The cost of production model can be used to estimate the minimum value of Bitcoin, based on the cost of mining.

- Ethereum: The NVT ratio model can be used to assess the value of the Ethereum network relative to the volume of transactions it processes.

- Stablecoins: The equation of exchange model can be used to estimate the value of stablecoins, based on their use in transactions.

- DeFi tokens: The DCF model can be used to value DeFi tokens, based on the future benefits they provide to holders.

By understanding these valuation models and how they are applied, you will be better equipped to assess the value of different tokens and make informed investment decisions.

In the next lesson, we will look at specific valuation models for utility tokens, security tokens, governance tokens, and NFTs.

7.5: Token Valuation for Utility Tokens

Understanding the Concept of Utility Tokens

Utility tokens, sometimes referred to as user tokens or app coins, represent future access to a company's product or service. The defining characteristic of utility tokens is that they are not designed as investments; if properly structured, this feature exempts utility tokens from federal laws governing securities.

By creating utility tokens, a startup can sell "digital coupons" for the service it is developing, much like electronics retailers accept pre-orders for video games that might not be released for several months. This is the primary function of utility tokens.

Factors Influencing the Value of Utility Tokens

The value of utility tokens is influenced by various factors. Here are some of the most significant ones:

1. **Demand for the Underlying Service:** If the service offered by the company is in high demand, it is likely that the value of the utility tokens will increase.

2. **Token Supply:** If the supply of tokens is limited, and demand is high, this can drive up the price of the tokens.

3. **Market Sentiment:** Like all cryptocurrencies, the value of utility tokens can be heavily influenced by market sentiment. Positive news can drive prices up, while negative news can drive prices down.

4. **Regulatory Environment:** The regulatory environment can also have a significant impact on the value of utility tokens. For example, if a government decides to

145

crack down on ICOs, this could negatively impact the value of utility tokens.

Valuation Models Applicable for Utility Tokens

Valuing utility tokens is complex due to their unique nature and the volatile market conditions. However, several models can be used to estimate their value:

1. Discounted Cash Flow (DCF): This model can be used if the utility token generates cash flow.

2. Comparable Analysis: This model compares the utility token with other similar tokens or assets.

3. Network Value to Transaction ratio (NVT): This model compares the value of the utility token's network to the transaction volume on the network.

4. Quantity Theory of Money: This model uses the equation $MV = PQ$, where M is the total supply of tokens, V is the velocity of the token, P is the price level, and Q is the index of real expenditures.

Each of these models has its strengths and weaknesses, and none of them can provide a definitive value. They should be used as tools to help estimate the potential value of a utility token.

Case Studies of Utility Token Valuation

Let's look at a few case studies to understand how utility tokens can be valued:

1. Ethereum (ETH): Ethereum's utility token, Ether, is used to fuel operations on the Ethereum network. The value of ETH is influenced by the demand for decentralized applications (dApps) and smart contracts on the Ethereum platform.

2. Binance Coin (BNB): Binance Coin is used to pay for fees within the Binance exchange. The value of BNB is influenced by the trading volume on the Binance exchange.

These case studies illustrate that the value of utility tokens is closely tied to the success and usage of the platform they are associated with.

In conclusion, utility token valuation is a complex process that requires a deep understanding of the underlying platform and market conditions. It's important to remember that the value of utility tokens can be highly volatile and unpredictable, and investors should proceed with caution.

"Crypto investing is like navigating uncharted waters – thrilling and unpredictable, yet full of potential for those who master its currents."
- Dennis Frank

7.6: Token Valuation for Security Tokens

Understanding the Concept of Security Tokens

Security tokens are a type of digital asset that falls within the regulatory purview of securities laws. They represent ownership in an external, tradable asset. Security tokens are subject to federal laws that govern securities, and failure to comply with these regulations can result in severe penalties.

Security tokens can represent a wide array of assets, including real estate, shares in a company, or participation in an investment fund. They offer a way to tokenize assets and put them on the blockchain, providing more transparency, efficiency, and accessibility than traditional securities.

Factors Influencing the Value of Security Tokens

Several factors can influence the value of security tokens:

1. **Underlying Asset Value:** Since security tokens represent ownership in an external asset, the value of that asset directly influences the token's value.

2. **Liquidity:** Security tokens can potentially be traded on a global scale, increasing their liquidity and, therefore, their value.

3. **Regulatory Compliance:** A security token that is fully compliant with regulatory requirements can attract more investors, thereby increasing its value.

4. **Token Utility:** If the token provides additional utility beyond just representing an asset (for example, voting rights or dividends), this can also increase its value.

5. **Market Sentiment:** The overall sentiment and behavior of investors in the market can greatly influence the value of security tokens.

Valuation Models Applicable for Security Tokens

Valuation of security tokens is a complex process due to the variety of assets they can represent and the regulatory landscape they navigate. However, some of the commonly used valuation models include:

1. **Discounted Cash Flow (DCF):** This model estimates the value of an investment based on its future cash flow. The DCF model can be used if the underlying asset of the security token generates cash flows.

2. **Net Asset Value (NAV):** This model is used when the security token represents an ownership interest in an investment fund. The NAV model values the token based on the total value of the fund's assets, minus any liabilities.

3. **Comparables Analysis:** This model is used when there are similar security tokens in the market. The value of the token is determined based on the valuation multiples of these comparable tokens.

Case Studies of Security Token Valuation

Let's look at some real-world examples of security token valuation:

Blockchain Capital (BCAP): BCAP is a security token that represents an ownership stake in a venture capital fund. The value of BCAP tokens is derived from the NAV of the fund's assets.

SPiCE VC: SPiCE VC is another security token that represents an ownership interest in a venture capital fund. The value of SPiCE VC tokens is based on the NAV of the fund's assets, and the token also provides additional utility in the form of profit-sharing.

In conclusion, security token valuation is a complex but crucial aspect of Tokenomics. Understanding the factors that influence the value of security tokens and the applicable valuation models can help investors make informed decisions and contribute to the overall health and growth of the token economy.

"In the cryptocurrency market, the dance of token pricing is a complex ballet, choreographed by supply, demand, utility, and the ever-shifting tides of economic and regulatory currents."
- Dennis Frank

7.7: Token Valuation for Governance Tokens and NFTs

In this lesson, we will delve into the valuation of two unique types of tokens - governance tokens and Non-Fungible Tokens (NFTs). Both token types have unique characteristics that influence their valuation in the market.

Understanding the Concept of Governance Tokens and NFTs

Governance Tokens are digital tokens that grant holders the right to vote on changes and decisions within a blockchain network or a decentralized application (dApp). They play a crucial role in decentralized finance (DeFi) and decentralized autonomous organizations (DAOs), enabling community-led decision-making.

Non-Fungible Tokens (NFTs), on the other hand, represent ownership or proof of authenticity of a unique item or piece of content. Unlike fungible tokens, which are identical to each other and can be exchanged on a one-to-one basis, NFTs are unique and cannot be exchanged on a like-for-like basis.

Factors Influencing the Value of Governance Tokens and NFTs

Several factors influence the value of Governance Tokens:

- **Network Participation:** The more active the network, the more valuable the governance token tends to be.

151

- **Voting Rights:** The power of the voting rights associated with the token can significantly affect its value.

- **Token Supply:** The total supply of the governance token and its distribution method can impact its market value.

The value of **NFTs** is influenced by:

- **Uniqueness:** Since NFTs represent unique assets, their rarity can significantly influence their value.

- **Ownership Rights:** The specific rights that come with the NFT, such as royalties from resales, can add to its value.

- **Demand:** The popularity of the asset the NFT represents can greatly affect its price.

Valuation Models Applicable for Governance Tokens and NFTs

Valuation models for both governance tokens and NFTs are still in their early stages of development. However, some commonly used methods include:

- **Discounted Cash Flow (DCF):** This model can be used for governance tokens that generate cash flows.

- **Comparables Analysis:** This involves comparing the token to similar tokens in the market.

- **Network Value to Transaction Ratio (NVT):** This model, like the P/E ratio in traditional finance, compares the network's value to the transaction volume on the network.

For NFTs, valuation is more subjective and often based on perceived value, like art or collectibles.

Case Studies of Governance Token and NFT Valuation

Let's look at two examples:

Uniswap (UNI): Uniswap's governance token, UNI, was distributed to users of the platform, and its value is derived from the voting rights it provides. The token has seen significant value appreciation due to the platform's popularity.

CryptoPunk NFTs: CryptoPunks are one of the earliest examples of NFTs. Each CryptoPunk is unique, and their value has skyrocketed, with some selling for millions of dollars, due to their rarity and the high demand among collectors.

In conclusion, the valuation of governance tokens and NFTs is a complex process influenced by various factors. As the market matures, more sophisticated valuation models are likely to emerge.

"Tokenomics is not just an economic model; it's a digital renaissance, painting the future of finance with strokes of code and creativity."- Dennis Frank

7.8: Future Trends in Token Valuation

Emerging Trends in Token Valuation

Token valuation is a dynamic field that is continuously evolving. As we move forward, we can expect to see several emerging trends that will shape the future of token valuation.

One such trend is the increasing use of data analytics and machine learning algorithms to predict token value. These advanced technologies can analyze vast amounts of data and identify patterns that humans might miss, leading to more accurate and reliable token valuations.

Another trend is the growing importance of community sentiment in token valuation. As the blockchain space becomes more democratized, the opinions and attitudes of the community are playing a larger role in determining the value of a token.

This is reflected in the rise of social listening tools that track and analyze discussions about a particular token on social media and other online platforms.

The Impact of DeFi and DAOs on Token Valuation

Decentralized Finance (DeFi) and Decentralized Autonomous Organizations (DAOs) are two significant developments in the blockchain space that are having a profound impact on token valuation.

DeFi refers to the use of blockchain technology to recreate and improve upon traditional financial systems, such as lending and borrowing, insurance, and asset trading.

DeFi tokens, which represent a stake in a DeFi project, are often valued based on the project's total value locked (TVL), a measure of the amount of assets deposited in the project.

DAOs, on the other hand, are organizations that are run by smart contracts on the blockchain, with decisions made through a voting process among token holders.

The value of a DAO's token can be influenced by factors such as the effectiveness of the DAO's governance, the success of its projects, and the level of participation by token holders.

The Intersection of Traditional Finance and Token Valuation

As blockchain technology becomes more mainstream, we are beginning to see a convergence of traditional finance and token valuation. This is evident in the increasing use of traditional financial valuation methods, such as discounted cash flow (DCF) and net present value (NPV), in token valuation.

Moreover, traditional financial institutions are starting to recognize the value of digital tokens. For example, some banks are now offering custody services for digital assets, and there are even ETFs that track the value of certain tokens. This recognition from traditional finance can lend legitimacy to digital tokens and potentially increase their value.

The Future of Token Valuation Models

Looking ahead, we can expect to see further evolution in token valuation models. As the blockchain space matures and more data becomes available, these models will likely become more sophisticated and accurate.

One area of potential growth is the use of multi-factor models that take into account a variety of factors in determining token value. These factors could include technical aspects of the block-chain project, such as its code quality and scalability, as well as external factors, such as regulatory developments and macroeconomic conditions.

In conclusion, the future of token valuation is likely to be characterized by increasing sophistication, the integration of traditional finance, and the growing influence of DeFi and DAOs.

As a participant in the blockchain space, staying abreast of these trends will be crucial to understanding and predicting the value of digital tokens.

"In the short run, the market is a voting machine but in the long run, it is a weighing machine."
- Benjamin Graham

7.9: Review and Analysis of Market Dynamics and Token Valuation

Recap of Key Concepts

In this module, we have delved deep into the world of market dynamics and token valuation. We started by understanding the market sentiment in tokenomics, which refers to the overall attitude of investors towards a particular token or the crypto market as a whole.

Market sentiment can be bullish (positive), bearish (negative), or neutral, and it plays a crucial role in influencing token prices.

We then explored the various factors influencing token pricing, such as supply and demand, market sentiment, technological advancements, regulatory news, and macroeconomic factors. Understanding these factors helps traders and investors make informed decisions.

Next, we discussed token valuation models. We learned that the valuation of utility tokens often involves assessing the current and future utility of the token within its ecosystem.

For security tokens, valuation can be similar to traditional financial assets and may involve analyzing future cash flows, dividends, or underlying assets.

Analysis and Discussion of Real-World Examples

Let's take a real-world example of Ethereum (ETH). Its price is influenced by various factors such as:

Supply and Demand: The more people want to buy ETH, the higher its price goes. Conversely, if more people want to sell ETH, its price drops.

Market Sentiment: Positive news or advancements in Ethereum's technology can lead to a bullish market sentiment, pushing the price up.

Technological Advancements: The transition of Ethereum from Proof-of-Work (PoW) to Proof-of-Stake (PoS) under Ethereum 2.0 has been a significant factor influencing its price.

Regulatory News: News about regulatory acceptance or crackdowns can significantly impact Ethereum's price.

In terms of valuation, Ethereum's utility within its ecosystem, particularly in DeFi applications and smart contracts, plays a significant role. The more utility ETH has, the higher its perceived value.

Interactive Assessment

Let's reinforce what we've learned with a short quiz:

What does bullish market sentiment mean?

A. The market sentiment is negative.

B. The market sentiment is positive.

C. The market sentiment is neutral.

Which of the following factors can influence token pricing?

A. Supply and Demand.

B. Market Sentiment.

C. Technological Advancements.

D. All of the above.

How is the valuation of utility tokens generally assessed?

A. By analyzing future cash flows.

B. By assessing the current and future utility of the token within its ecosystem.

C. By analyzing underlying assets.

Final Thoughts

Understanding market dynamics and token valuation is crucial in tokenomics. It helps traders, investors, and even token issuers navigate the complex world of cryptocurrencies.

As we move forward, keep in mind that market dynamics and token valuation are influenced by a myriad of factors, and they can change rapidly. Therefore, continuous learning and staying updated with the latest trends and news is key to mastering tokenomics.

"The four most expensive words in the English language are, 'This time it's different."
- Sir John Templeton

8.1: Understanding the Utility of Tokens

Introduction to the Concept of Token Utility

Token utility refers to the functional use or purpose that a token serves within its native ecosystem. It is the reason a token exists and what it can be used for. Utility tokens are not created as investments; instead, they are meant to be used within a specific blockchain ecosystem, often providing access to a service, or acting as a form of currency within the system.

Tokens as a Medium of Exchange in Blockchain Ecosystems

In many blockchain ecosystems, tokens serve as a medium of exchange, facilitating transactions and interactions within the network. These tokens can be used to purchase goods or services, participate in network governance, or access specific features of the platform. For example, Ether (ETH) is used as a form of payment for transactions and computational services on the Ethereum network.

The Role of Tokens in Incentivizing Network Participation

Tokens can also play a crucial role in incentivizing participation and behavior within a blockchain network. By rewarding network participants with tokens, the network can encourage desired behaviors such as validating transactions, contributing to the development of the platform, or promoting the network. For instance, Bitcoin miners are rewarded with BTC for validating transactions and adding them to the blockchain.

The Use of Tokens for Staking and Securing Blockchain Networks

Staking is another key utility of tokens in many blockchain networks. In Proof-of-Stake (PoS) and Delegated Proof-of-Stake (DPoS) systems, network participants can 'stake' their tokens as a form of collateral in order to validate transactions and secure the network.

Staking tokens helps to ensure that validators act in the best interest of the network, as they stand to lose their staked tokens if they act dishonestly.

Case Studies of Utility Tokens in Real-World Applications

There are numerous examples of utility tokens in real-world applications. For instance, Binance Coin (BNB) can be used to pay for transaction fees on the Binance exchange, participate in token sales on the Binance launchpad, and more.

Another example is Filecoin (FIL), which is used as a payment method for storage and retrieval of data in the Filecoin network.

In conclusion, the utility of tokens is a fundamental aspect of Tokenomics. Understanding how tokens function within their respective ecosystems can provide valuable insights into the design and economic models of blockchain networks.

8.2: Tokens in Governance and Decision Making

Introduction to Decentralized Autonomous Organizations (DAOs)

Decentralized Autonomous Organizations (DAOs) are one of the most revolutionary concepts in the blockchain world. DAOs are organizations that are completely run by smart contracts, with no central authority.

This means that all decisions are made by the community through a democratic voting process, which is facilitated by governance tokens.

The Role of Governance Tokens in DAOs

Governance tokens play a crucial role in DAOs. They give holders the right to vote on proposals and make decisions about the future direction of the organization.

The more tokens a person holds, the more voting power they have. This is a way of ensuring that those who have a larger stake in the organization have a greater say in its operation.

The Process of Decision Making in DAOs Using Tokens

The decision-making process in DAOs using tokens typically follows these steps:

Proposal Submission: Any token holder can submit a proposal for a change or new feature in the DAO. This could be anything from changing a protocol parameter to funding a new project.

Discussion: Once a proposal is submitted, there is usually a period of discussion where token holders can debate the merits of the proposal.

Voting: After the discussion period, token holders vote on the proposal. Each token represents one vote, and the proposal is accepted or rejected based on the majority of votes.

Execution: If the proposal is accepted, the changes are automatically implemented through the DAO's smart contract.

Pros and Cons of Token-Based Governance

Token-based governance has several advantages. It is transparent and democratic and allows for community participation.

However, it also has its drawbacks. It can lead to plutocracy, where those with more tokens have more power. It can also lead to low voter turnout if token holders are not actively engaged.

Case Studies of Successful DAOs and Their Governance Models

There are several successful DAOs that use token-based governance. Here are a few examples:

MakerDAO: MakerDAO is a decentralized lending platform that allows users to borrow and lend cryptocurrencies. It uses a governance token called MKR. MKR holders can vote on changes to the system, like the addition of new collateral types or changes to system parameters.

Compound: Compound is a DeFi lending platform. It uses a governance token called COMP. COMP holders can propose and vote on changes to the protocol.

Uniswap: Uniswap is a decentralized exchange protocol. It uses a governance token called UNI. UNI holders can vote on changes to the protocol, like fee structures or token listings.

In conclusion, tokens play a vital role in the governance and decision-making process of DAOs. They provide a democratic and transparent way for community members to participate in the organization's operation.

However, like any system, it is not without its challenges, and continuous improvements and adjustments are needed to ensure its fairness and effectiveness.

Buy not on optimism, but on arithmetic." - Benjamin Graham

8.3: Tokens in Decentralized Finance (DeFi) Applications

Understanding the Concept of DeFi

Decentralized Finance, commonly known as DeFi, is a block-chain-based form of finance that does not rely on central financial intermediaries such as brokerages, exchanges, or banks to offer traditional financial instruments.

Instead, it utilizes smart contracts on blockchain, the most common being Ethereum. DeFi platforms allow people to lend or borrow funds from others, speculate on price movements on a range of assets using derivatives, trade cryptocurrencies, insure against risks, and earn interest in savings-like accounts.

The Role of Tokens in DeFi Applications

Tokens play a pivotal role in the DeFi ecosystem. They serve as a medium of exchange, a store of value, or a unit of account. Tokens are used for various purposes in DeFi applications, including governance, incentivizing user participation, and earning rewards. They are also used to represent digital assets that can be traded on the platform.

Different Types of Tokens in DeFi

There are several types of tokens used in DeFi applications:

Stablecoins: These are digital tokens that are pegged to a stable asset, like the US dollar. They are often used in DeFi applications to reduce the volatility typically associated with cryptocurrencies.

Governance Tokens: These tokens give holders the right to vote on changes to a platform's rules and parameters. They are a key component of decentralized governance in DeFi applications.

165

Liquidity Tokens: These tokens are provided as proof of providing liquidity to a liquidity pool. They can be used to claim a proportionate share of the pool's total assets and any trading fees generated by the pool.

The Use of Tokens in Yield Farming and Liquidity Mining

Yield farming and liquidity mining are popular strategies in DeFi that involve lending or providing liquidity to earn rewards.

In yield farming, users lend their assets to a DeFi platform. In return, they receive interest and additional tokens as rewards. The tokens can be governance tokens, which gives the yield farmers a say in the future development of the DeFi platform.

In liquidity mining, users provide liquidity to a DeFi platform's liquidity pool. They receive liquidity tokens as a reward, which can be redeemed for a share of the pool's total assets and trading fees.

Case Studies of DeFi Projects and Their Token Models

Compound: Compound is a DeFi lending platform that allows users to earn interest on their cryptocurrencies by depositing them into one of several pools supported by the platform. Users can also borrow against their deposited assets. Compound's native token, COMP, is a governance token that is distributed to users of the protocol.

Uniswap: Uniswap is a decentralized exchange protocol built on Ethereum. It uses an automated liquidity protocol. Users can trade directly with the smart contract on the platform. The platform's native token, UNI, is a governance token that was initially distributed to users of the protocol.

Yearn.finance: Yearn.finance is a DeFi platform that provides yield farming strategies to its users. It automatically moves users' funds between different lending protocols to maximize returns. Its native token, YFI, is a governance token that was distributed to users who provided liquidity to the platform's pools.

By understanding the role and functionality of tokens in DeFi applications, we can better appreciate the innovative solutions these platforms provide in the world of finance.

As we move forward, the utility and functionality of tokens are expected to evolve and expand, further pushing the boundaries of what's possible in the DeFi space.

"Speculation is most dangerous when it looks easiest."
- Warren Buffett

8.4:Non-Fungible Tokens (NFTs) and Their Functionality

Introduction to Non-Fungible Tokens (NFTs)

Non-Fungible Tokens (NFTs) are a unique type of token in the blockchain ecosystem. Unlike cryptocurrencies like Bitcoin or Ethereum, which are fungible and can be exchanged on a one-to-one basis, NFTs are unique and cannot be exchanged on a like-for-like basis. Each NFT has a unique identifier that distinguishes it from every other token, making it one-of-a-kind.

The Unique Properties and Functionalities of NFTs

NFTs possess unique properties that set them apart from other types of digital tokens. They are:

Uniqueness: Each NFT is unique and cannot be replicated, making it a perfect tool for representing ownership of unique items or assets.

Indivisibility: Unlike cryptocurrencies, which can be divided into smaller units (like 0.01 BTC), NFTs cannot be divided and must be bought, sold, or traded as a whole.

Interoperability: NFTs are typically built on standard protocols (like ERC-721 or ERC-1155 on the Ethereum blockchain) allowing them to be easily traded and stored in various wallets and platforms.

The Use of NFTs in Digital Art, Collectibles, and Virtual Real Estate

One of the most popular use cases of NFTs is in the realm of digital art and collectibles. Artists can mint their artwork as NFTs, providing a blockchain-based proof of ownership that can be bought, sold, or traded on various platforms.

This has opened up new monetization avenues for digital artists and has led to the explosion of digital art marketplaces like OpenSea, Rarible, and Foundation.

Similarly, NFTs have found a place in the world of digital collectibles. Projects like CryptoKitties and NBA Top Shot have popularized the concept of blockchain-based collectibles, where each item or 'moment' is a unique NFT.

Virtual real estate is another emerging field where NFTs are making a mark. Platforms like Decentraland and Cryptovoxels allow users to buy, sell, and trade parcels of virtual land as NFTs.

The Role of NFTs in Proving Ownership and Provenance

One of the key functionalities of NFTs is their ability to prove ownership and provenance. When an NFT is minted, it is associated with a specific owner (the wallet address of the minter).

This ownership record is immutable and transparent, making it easy to verify who owns a particular NFT.

Similarly, the history of an NFT (including its creation and all subsequent transactions) is recorded on the blockchain, providing a clear and indisputable record of its provenance.

Case Studies of Successful NFT Projects and Their Impact on the Digital Economy

There have been several successful NFT projects that have had a significant impact on the digital economy. Perhaps the most famous is Beeple's digital art piece "Everydays: The First 5000 Days," which was minted as an NFT and sold for a staggering $69 million at Christie's auction house.

CryptoPunks, one of the first NFT projects on the Ethereum blockchain, has also seen massive success, with individual punks selling for millions of dollars.

These projects have not only demonstrated the potential of NFTs to disrupt traditional industries like art and collectibles but have also sparked a wider conversation about the value and ownership of digital assets.

In conclusion, NFTs are a powerful tool in the blockchain ecosystem, with unique properties and functionalities that make them ideal for representing ownership of unique digital assets.

As the technology matures, we can expect to see even more innovative uses of NFTs across various sectors.

"Risk comes from not knowing what you're doing."
- Warren Buffet

8.5: Token Functionality and Interoperability

Understanding the Concept of Token Interoperability

Token interoperability is a crucial aspect of the blockchain eco-system. It refers to the ability of a token to interact and operate across multiple blockchain platforms.

This interoperability is vital as it allows for seamless transactions and data exchange between different blockchain networks, thereby enhancing the overall functionality of tokens.

The Role of Tokens in Enabling Cross-Chain Transactions

Tokens play a pivotal role in enabling cross-chain transactions. Cross-chain transactions refer to the transfer of tokens or data from one blockchain network to another.

This is made possible through the use of interoperable tokens, which can be transferred across different networks while maintaining their original properties and functionalities.

For instance, a token created on the Ethereum network can be transferred to the Binance Smart Chain network without any loss of functionality. This cross-chain operability of tokens has opened up new possibilities for blockchain technology, enabling a more interconnected and interoperable blockchain ecosystem.

The Use of Wrapped Tokens for Bridging Different Blockchain Networks

One common method of achieving token interoperability is through the use of wrapped tokens. A wrapped token is a type of token that represents another token on a different blockchain. It's essentially a bridge between two different blockchain networks.

For example, Wrapped Bitcoin (WBTC) is a token on the Ethereum blockchain that represents Bitcoin. It allows Bitcoin to be used within the Ethereum ecosystem, thus bridging the two separate blockchain networks.

This is achieved by locking up the original token (in this case, Bitcoin) in a smart contract and then issuing the equivalent amount of the wrapped token on the other blockchain.

The Challenges and Solutions in Achieving Token Interoperability

Despite the potential benefits, achieving token interoperability is not without challenges. These challenges include technical complexities, security risks, and regulatory concerns.

Technical complexities arise from the fact that different blockchain networks have different protocols, consensus mechanisms, and smart contract functionalities. Security risks stem from the fact that cross-chain transactions often involve third-party intermediaries, which could be vulnerable to attacks.

 To overcome these challenges, various solutions have been proposed and implemented. These include the development of blockchain interoperability platforms like Polkadot and Cosmos, the use of decentralized exchanges for cross-chain swaps, and the creation of multi-chain wallets that can hold tokens from different blockchains.

Future Trends in Token Functionality and Interoperability

Looking ahead, token functionality and interoperability are expected to play an increasingly important role in the blockchain ecosystem. As more and more blockchain networks emerge, the need for interoperability will only grow.

In the future, we can expect to see more advanced solutions for token interoperability, including the development of universal standards for cross-chain transactions, the integration of artificial intelligence for enhanced security, and the proliferation of decentralized finance (DeFi) applications that leverage interoperable tokens.

In conclusion, token interoperability is a key aspect of the blockchain ecosystem that enhances the functionality of tokens and enables seamless cross-chain transactions.

Despite the challenges, various solutions are being developed to promote interoperability, pointing to a future where tokens can freely interact and operate across multiple blockchain networks.

"An investment in knowledge always pays the best interest."
- Benjamin Franklin

8.6: Token Utility and Functionality: Risks and Challenges

Understanding the Risks Associated with Token Utility and Functionality

While tokens bring about a myriad of benefits in the blockchain ecosystem, they are not without risks. The utility and functionality of tokens can be compromised by various factors, including technological vulnerabilities, market volatility, and regulatory uncertainties.

For instance, a token's utility can be undermined if the platform it operates on has security flaws, leading to potential hacking incidents. Similarly, the functionality of a token can be affected by market volatility, as drastic price fluctuations can deter users from adopting the token for transactions or other uses.

The Challenges in Designing Effective Token Models

Designing an effective token model is a complex task that requires a deep understanding of both the technical and economic aspects of the blockchain.

One of the main challenges is to create a token that incentivizes positive behavior among users while discouraging malicious activities. This involves careful consideration of the token's distribution mechanism, its role within the ecosystem, and the economic incentives it provides.

Furthermore, the token model must be flexible enough to adapt to changing market conditions and user needs, yet robust enough to maintain its core functionality and value proposition.

The Impact of Regulatory Frameworks on Token Utility

Regulatory frameworks can significantly impact the utility and functionality of tokens. In some jurisdictions, tokens may be classified as securities and subject to stringent regulations, which can limit their utility and functionality.

For instance, security tokens may not be used as a medium of exchange in the same way as utility tokens due to regulatory restrictions. Additionally, regulatory uncertainties can deter potential users and investors, affecting the token's market adoption and valuation.

The Risk of Token Concentration and Its Impact on Network Security

Token concentration refers to the scenario where a large portion of tokens is held by a small number of users. This can pose a significant risk to the network's security and functionality.

For instance, in a Proof-of-Stake (PoS) blockchain, users with a large number of tokens have more voting power, which can lead to centralization and potential manipulation of the network.

Similarly, token concentration can create market manipulation risks, as large token holders can influence the token's price to their advantage.

Mitigation Strategies for Managing Risks Associated with Token Utility and Functionality

To manage the risks associated with token utility and functionality, several mitigation strategies can be employed. For instance, to address technological risks, rigorous security audits and testing should be conducted before the token's launch.

To mitigate market risks, a well-designed token economic model that balances supply and demand can help stabilize the token's price. Regulatory risks can be managed through legal consultation and compliance with relevant laws and regulations.

Finally, to prevent token concentration, a fair and transparent token distribution mechanism can be implemented.

In conclusion, while tokens offer innovative ways to facilitate transactions and incentivize user behavior in the blockchain ecosystem, they also come with various risks and challenges.

Understanding these risks and implementing effective mitigation strategies is crucial for the successful deployment and operation of token-based systems.

The stock market is a device for transferring money from the impatient to the patient."
- Warren Buffet

8.7: The Future of Token Utility and Functionality

In this lesson, we will explore the future of token utility and functionality. We will delve into emerging trends, the role of tokens in Web 3.0, the future of NFTs, the potential impact of Central Bank Digital Currencies (CBDCs), and predictions for the evolution of token utility and functionality in the next decade.

Emerging Trends in Token Utility and Functionality

As the blockchain ecosystem evolves, so does the utility and functionality of tokens. Tokens are no longer just a medium of exchange or a store of value. They are now being used for governance, staking, yield farming, and to access exclusive services within a specific ecosystem.

In the future, we can expect tokens to have even more complex functionalities. For example, tokens could be used to represent fractional ownership of physical assets, or to access personalized services based on user preferences and behavior.

The Role of Tokens in Web 3.0 and the Decentralized Internet

Web 3.0, also known as the decentralized internet, is a vision for a new generation of the internet that is built on blockchain technology. In this vision, tokens play a crucial role. They are used to incentivize network participants, facilitate transactions, and enable decentralized governance. As Web 3.0 continues to develop, we can expect tokens to become even more integral to its functioning.

For example, tokens could be used to reward users for contributing data, to facilitate peer-to-peer transactions without intermediaries, or to enable decentralized decision-making in online communities.

The Future of NFTs and Their Potential Uses

Non-Fungible Tokens (NFTs) have gained significant attention in recent years due to their ability to represent unique digital assets. NFTs have been used for digital art, music, virtual real estate, and more.

In the future, the use cases for NFTs could expand even further. For example, NFTs could be used to represent ownership of real-world assets like houses or cars, to create personalized digital experiences, or to enable new forms of digital identity.

The Potential Impact of Central Bank Digital Currencies (CBDCs) on Token Utility

Central Bank Digital Currencies (CBDCs) are a new type of digital currency that is being explored by various central banks around the world. CBDCs could potentially have a significant impact on the utility and functionality of tokens.

For example, if a CBDC were to be widely adopted, it could potentially serve as a stable medium of exchange within the blockchain ecosystem, reducing the need for stablecoins. On the other hand, CBDCs could also compete with existing tokens for certain use cases, such as payments or remittances.

Predictions for the Evolution of Token Utility and Functionality in the Next Decade

Looking ahead, we can expect the utility and functionality of tokens to continue to evolve in exciting ways.

As blockchain technology matures and becomes more widely adopted, tokens could become a fundamental part of our digital lives.

We might see tokens being used to represent all sorts of digital and physical assets, to facilitate a wide range of transactions, and to enable new forms of online interaction and collaboration. The possibilities are truly endless, and we are just at the beginning of this exciting journey.

In the next lesson, we will delve deeper into the emerging trends and the future of Tokenomics.

Key Takeaways:

- The utility and functionality of tokens are expected to evolve as the blockchain ecosystem matures.

- Tokens will play a crucial role in Web 3.0 and the decentralized internet.

- The use cases for NFTs are expected to expand significantly in the future.

- Central Bank Digital Currencies (CBDCs) could potentially impact the utility and functionality of tokens.

- The next decade will see an exciting evolution in the utility and functionality of tokens.

9.1: The Role of Tokenomics in DeFi and Yield Farming

Understanding the concept of DeFi and Yield Farming

Decentralized Finance, or DeFi, is a blockchain-based form of finance that does not rely on central financial intermediaries such as brokerages, exchanges, or banks to offer traditional financial instruments. Instead, it utilizes smart contracts on blockchains, the most common being Ethereum.

Yield Farming, also referred to as liquidity mining, is a way to generate rewards with cryptocurrency holdings. In simple terms, it means locking up cryptocurrencies and getting rewards.

In the context of DeFi, yield farming can be directly compared to staking. However, it's a bit more complex due to the usage of multiple DeFi platforms.

The role of tokens in DeFi and Yield Farming

Tokens play a crucial role in DeFi and yield farming. They are used as a medium of exchange, a store of value, and a unit of account. In DeFi, tokens are often used to represent ownership or participation rights.

They can be staked to earn rewards, used as collateral for loans, or to vote on governance decisions within the DeFi ecosystem.

In yield farming, participants earn rewards in the form of additional tokens. These rewards can come from a single DeFi platform or multiple platforms.

The more tokens a yield farmer has, the more they can potentially earn. This incentivizes participants to supply more tokens to the DeFi ecosystem.

Case studies: Successful use of Tokenomics in DeFi and Yield Farming

Uniswap: Uniswap is a decentralized exchange protocol built on Ethereum. In Uniswap, users can swap tokens, provide liquidity by staking tokens, and earn fees in return. Uniswap has its native token, UNI, which is used for governance decisions within the Uniswap ecosystem. The distribution of UNI tokens to users and liquidity providers has been a successful example of tokenomics in DeFi.

Compound: Compound is a DeFi lending protocol that allows users to earn interest on their cryptocurrencies by depositing them into one of several pools supported by the platform. Compound's native token, COMP, is used for governance decisions, and users can earn COMP tokens by interacting with the Compound protocol.

Future trends in DeFi and Yield Farming

The DeFi and yield farming space is continuously evolving, with new protocols and tokens being launched regularly. Here are a few trends to look out for:

Interoperability: As the DeFi ecosystem grows, there will be an increased need for different DeFi platforms to interact and communicate with each other seamlessly. This will lead to the development of more cross-chain solutions and interoperable DeFi platforms.

Regulation: As DeFi becomes more mainstream, it is likely to attract more attention from regulators. This could lead to more clarity and guidelines around DeFi and yield farming, which could help to further legitimize and stabilize the sector.

Innovation in Yield Farming Strategies: As more people get involved in yield farming, there will be more innovation in yield farming strategies. This could include new ways to optimize returns, mitigate risks, and automate yield farming strategies.

In conclusion, tokenomics plays a vital role in the functioning and success of DeFi and yield farming. Understanding tokenomics can help users to better navigate the DeFi ecosystem and make more informed decisions.

"Case studies are the compasses of learning, guiding us through the real-world complexities, illuminating paths of wisdom in uncharted territories." – Dennis Frank

9.2: The Rise of DAOs and Community Governance in Tokenomics

Introduction to Decentralized Autonomous Organizations (DAOs)

Decentralized Autonomous Organizations (DAOs) are a revolutionary concept in the blockchain ecosystem. They are organizations governed by smart contracts on the blockchain, with decision-making power distributed among token holders.

DAOs operate without centralized authority, and their rules are transparent and immutable. They represent a new model of organizational governance that is open, democratic, and resistant to censorship.

DAOs have gained significant attention in the blockchain and cryptocurrency space due to their potential to disrupt traditional organizational structures.

They can be used for a wide range of applications, from decentralized finance (DeFi) platforms to community-governed social networks.

The Role of Tokens in DAOs and Community Governance

Tokens play a crucial role in DAOs and community governance. They are used as a means of representing voting power within the organization. Token holders can propose changes to the organization's rules, vote on proposals, and even fund projects.

This creates a democratic system where the direction of the organization is determined by its community.

The use of tokens in DAOs also incentivizes active participation from the community. By owning tokens, members have a vested interest in the success of the organization. This can lead to more active engagement and better decision-making.

Case Studies: Successful Use of Tokenomics in DAOs

There are several examples of successful DAOs that have effectively utilized tokenomics. One such example is MakerDAO, a decentralized lending platform on the Ethereum blockchain.

MakerDAO is governed by its token holders, who vote on various aspects of the platform, such as the stability fee and the debt ceiling. The MKR token represents voting rights in the MakerDAO system, and its holders are responsible for managing the Maker Protocol's risks.

Another example is the decentralized exchange Uniswap, which introduced its own governance token, UNI, in 2020. UNI token holders can vote on changes to the platform, including its fee structure and the introduction of new features.

Future Trends in DAOs and Community Governance

The rise of DAOs and community governance is an exciting trend in the blockchain space. As more people become aware of the benefits of decentralized governance, we can expect to see more DAOs being created.

This could lead to a shift in how organizations are structured and governed, with more emphasis on community involvement and democratic decision-making.

Furthermore, as blockchain technology continues to evolve, we may see new types of DAOs with even more advanced features. For example, DAOs could incorporate machine learning algorithms to automate certain aspects of decision-making. They could also use prediction markets to gauge community sentiment and make more informed decisions.

In conclusion, DAOs and community governance represent a significant trend in tokenomics. They demonstrate the potential of blockchain technology to create more open and democratic organizations, and they are likely to play a crucial role in the future of the blockchain ecosystem.

"In a world woven with binary threads, every bit of knowledge unlocks a universe of possibilities. Navigate the digital expanse with curiosity, and let every click be a step towards mastering the unknown." - Dennis Frank

9.3: Intersection of Tokenomics and Traditional Finance

Understanding the Relationship Between Tokenomics and Traditional Finance

Tokenomics, the economic system that governs the functioning of digital tokens, has a profound impact on traditional finance.

Traditional finance, which is based on centralized banking systems and government-issued currencies, is being challenged by the decentralized, peer-to-peer nature of cryptocurrencies and blockchain technology.

In the traditional financial system, banks and other financial institutions function as intermediaries, facilitating transactions and ensuring the stability of the financial system.

In contrast, Tokenomics operates on blockchain technology, eliminating the need for intermediaries and enabling direct, peer-to-peer transactions.

This fundamental difference has significant implications for the functioning of financial markets, the nature of financial instruments, and the structure of financial institutions.

How Tokenomics is Changing Traditional Finance

Tokenomics is changing traditional finance in several ways:

1. **Decentralization:** Blockchain technology, the backbone of Tokenomics, is inherently decentralized. This decentralization disrupts the centralized nature of traditional finance, enabling peer-to-peer transactions and reducing the need for intermediaries.

2. **Tokenization:** Tokenomics allows for the tokenization of assets, meaning any asset (real estate, art, company shares) can be represented as digital tokens on a block-chain. This opens up new possibilities for asset ownership and investment, making them more accessible and liquid.

3. **Smart Contracts:** Tokenomics leverages smart contracts, which are self-executing contracts with the terms of the agreement directly written into code. Smart contracts automate and streamline financial transactions, reducing the need for manual intervention and the potential for human error.

Case Studies: Successful Integration of Tokenomics in Traditional Finance

Several companies and projects have successfully integrated Tokenomics into traditional finance:

1. **DeFi Projects:** Decentralized Finance (DeFi) projects like Compound and Aave have used Tokenomics to create lending platforms that operate without intermediaries. Users can lend and borrow directly from each other, earning interest on their deposits.

2. **Security Tokens:** Platforms like Polymath have used Tokenomics to create security tokens, which represent ownership in real-world assets like real estate or company shares. These tokens are subject to securities regulations, bridging the gap between blockchain and traditional finance.

3. **Stablecoins:** Stablecoins like Tether (USDT) and USD Coin (USDC) have used Tokenomics to create digital tokens that are pegged to the value of traditional currencies. These stablecoins combine the benefits of cryptocurrencies (speed, transparency, security) with the stability of traditional currencies.

Future Trends at the Intersection of Tokenomics and Traditional Finance

As Tokenomics continues to evolve, it is expected to further integrate with traditional finance:

1. **Regulation:** As Tokenomics becomes more mainstream, it is likely to face increased regulation. This could lead to more transparency and stability in the cryptocurrency market, making it more attractive to traditional investors.

2. **Institutional Adoption:** More financial institutions are expected to adopt blockchain technology and Tokenomics. This could lead to the creation of new financial products and services that combine the benefits of blockchain with the stability and trust of traditional finance.

3. **Interoperability:** As more assets become tokenized, there will be a need for interoperability between different blockchains and traditional financial systems. This could lead to the development of new technologies and standards that facilitate cross-chain and cross-platform transactions.

In conclusion, the intersection of Tokenomics and traditional finance is a rapidly evolving field, offering exciting opportunities and challenges. As we continue to explore this intersection, we can expect to see further disruption and innovation in the world of finance.

9.4: The Impact of Regulation on the Future of Tokenomics

In this lesson, we will delve into the impact of regulation on the future of Tokenomics. We will explore the current regulatory landscape for tokens, discuss the potential influence of future regulations on Tokenomics, and examine case studies of how regulation has shaped Tokenomics in the past. We will conclude with a look at future trends in regulation and Tokenomics.

Understanding the Current Regulatory Landscape for Tokens

Regulation is a key factor that shapes the landscape of Tokenomics. Currently, there is a wide range of regulatory approaches towards digital tokens across the globe.

Some jurisdictions have embraced digital tokens and blockchain technology, providing clear regulatory guidelines for token issuance and management.

Others have taken a more cautious approach, imposing strict regulations or outright bans on certain activities related to digital tokens.

The regulatory landscape is complex and constantly evolving, with regulators trying to strike a balance between fostering innovation and protecting consumers and investors. Key regulatory considerations include anti-money laundering (AML) and know your customer (KYC) requirements, securities laws, and tax implications.

The Possible Impact of Future Regulations on Tokenomics

Future regulations can significantly influence the development and adoption of digital tokens. Stricter regulations may limit the scope of Tokenomics by imposing stringent requirements on token issuance and management.

On the other hand, clear and supportive regulatory frameworks can foster the growth of Tokenomics by providing certainty and reducing risk for participants.

Regulations can also shape the design and functionality of tokens. For example, regulatory requirements can influence decisions about token distribution mechanisms, incentive structures, and governance models.

Future regulations may also address emerging trends in Tokenomics, such as decentralized finance (DeFi) and non-fungible tokens (NFTs).

Case Studies: How Regulation Has Shaped Tokenomics in the Past

Regulation has already had a significant impact on Tokenomics in the past. For instance, the introduction of securities laws to digital tokens has led to the emergence of security tokens, which represent ownership in an underlying asset and are subject to securities regulations.

Another example is the impact of AML and KYC regulations on initial coin offerings (ICOs). These regulations have led to changes in ICO practices, including increased transparency and the implementation of KYC procedures.

Future Trends in Regulation and Tokenomics

Looking ahead, we can expect continued evolution in the regulatory landscape for digital tokens. Regulators are likely to continue grappling with the challenges posed by decentralized, borderless token ecosystems.

We may see more regulatory clarity and harmonization across jurisdictions, which could facilitate the global growth of Tokenomics.

Emerging trends such as DeFi and NFTs will also bring new regulatory challenges. Regulators will need to understand these trends and adapt their frameworks accordingly.

The future of Tokenomics will be significantly influenced by how regulators respond to these challenges.

In conclusion, regulation plays a crucial role in shaping the future of Tokenomics. By understanding the regulatory landscape, participants can better navigate the world of digital tokens and contribute to the development of Tokenomics.

In the next lesson, we will explore the role of Tokenomics in the future of blockchain technology.

Key Takeaways:

- The regulatory landscape for digital tokens is complex and constantly evolving.

- Future regulations can significantly impact the development and adoption of digital tokens.

- Regulation has already shaped Tokenomics in significant ways, as seen in the case studies of securities laws and AML/KYC regulations.

- Regulatory trends, including regulatory responses to emerging trends like DeFi and NFTs will significantly influence the future of Tokenomics.

9.5: The Role of Tokenomics in the Future Blockchain Technology

Understanding the Importance of Tokenomics in Blockchain Technology

Tokenomics plays a pivotal role in the evolution and functionality of blockchain technology. It serves as the economic framework that allows blockchain networks to operate efficiently.

The design and implementation of tokens within a blockchain ecosystem can influence user behavior, incentivize participation, and facilitate transactions.

In essence, Tokenomics is the lifeblood of blockchain technology, providing the necessary economic incentives for the system to function and thrive.

How Tokenomics is Driving Innovation in Blockchain Technology

Tokenomics has been a key driver for innovation in the blockchain space. It has allowed for the creation of decentralized applications (dApps), decentralized finance (DeFi) platforms, and various other blockchain-based solutions.

For instance, by creating utility tokens, blockchain projects can incentivize user participation and engagement. These tokens often provide users with access to specific services within the ecosystem, or they can be used to reward users for contributing to the network.

Security tokens, on the other hand, can represent ownership in an asset, allowing for the tokenization of real world assets like real estate or art. This has opened up new possibilities for asset management and investment.

Governance tokens have enabled decentralized governance models, where token holders can vote on proposals and influence the direction of the project.

This has fostered a sense of community ownership and participation, which is a key aspect of many successful blockchain projects.

Case Studies: Successful Use of Tokenomics in Blockchain Innovation

Case Study 1: Ethereum

Ethereum is a prime example of the successful use of Tokenomics in blockchain innovation. Its native token, Ether (ETH), is used to incentivize miners to secure the network and validate transactions.

Furthermore, ETH is used to pay for transaction fees (known as gas) within the network, creating a demand for the token and ensuring its utility.

Case Study 2: MakerDAO

MakerDAO, a decentralized autonomous organization (DAO) on the Ethereum blockchain, uses a dual-token system (MKR and DAI) to maintain the stability of its decentralized stablecoin.

MKR token holders have governance rights, allowing them to vote on proposals and make decisions about the system's parameters. DAI, on the other hand, is a stablecoin pegged to the US dollar, providing stability in the volatile crypto market.

Future Trends in Blockchain Technology and Tokenomics

As blockchain technology continues to evolve, so too will the role of Tokenomics. Here are a few potential trends:

Increased Tokenization of Assets: As the benefits of tokenization become more apparent, we can expect to see an increase in the tokenization of real-world assets. This could potentially disrupt traditional industries like real estate, art, and finance.

More Sophisticated Economic Models: As projects experiment with different token models and economic structures, we are likely to see more sophisticated and innovative approaches to Tokenomics.

Regulatory Developments: As the blockchain space matures, regulatory clarity will become increasingly important. This could have a significant impact on Tokenomics, particularly in relation to security tokens and ICOs.

Integration with Traditional Finance: As blockchain technology becomes more mainstream, we may see more integration with traditional finance. This could lead to new token models and use cases, further driving innovation in the space.

In conclusion, the role of Tokenomics in the future of blockchain technology is crucial. By understanding and leveraging Tokenomics, blockchain projects can drive user engagement, incentivize participation, and create innovative solutions that could potentially disrupt various industries.

9.6: The Future of Token Creation and Distribution Mechanisms

Understanding the Current State of Token Creation and Distribution Mechanisms

In the current state of Tokenomics, token creation and distribution mechanisms play a critical role in the overall functioning of a blockchain ecosystem.

These mechanisms, which include Initial Coin Offerings (ICOs), Security Token Offerings (STOs), Airdrops, and Forks, among others, are used to introduce new tokens into the market and distribute them to users.

ICOs, for instance, have been a popular method for blockchain startups to raise funds by selling their tokens to investors. STOs, on the other hand, offer tokens that represent an underlying asset, providing investors with an equity stake in the company.

Airdrops are used to distribute tokens to existing holders, often to promote a new project or reward loyal users. Forks, meanwhile, create a new version of an existing blockchain, often leading to the creation of new tokens.

How Emerging Trends are Shaping the Future of Token Creation and Distribution

Emerging trends in the blockchain and cryptocurrency space are shaping the future of token creation and distribution mechanisms. For instance, the rise of Decentralized Finance (DeFi) has led to the creation of new types of tokens, such as yield farming tokens, which are earned by providing liquidity to DeFi protocols.

Another trend is the increasing use of DAOs (Decentralized Autonomous Organizations) for token distribution. DAOs are organizations that are run by smart contracts on the blockchain, enabling a democratic and transparent distribution of tokens.

Moreover, regulatory developments are also influencing the future of token creation and distribution. As governments around the world start to recognize and regulate cryptocurrencies, we may see more regulated and compliant token distribution mechanisms, such as regulated STOs.

Case Studies: Innovative Token Creation and Distribution Mechanisms

Case Study 1: Uniswap and Liquidity Mining
Uniswap, a popular DeFi protocol, introduced an innovative token distribution mechanism called liquidity mining.

Users who provide liquidity to Uniswap's trading pools earn UNI tokens as a reward. This mechanism not only incentivizes users to contribute to the protocol's liquidity but also ensures a fair and decentralized distribution of tokens.

Case Study 2: The Graph and its Curator Program
The Graph, a decentralized protocol for indexing and querying data from blockchains, introduced a unique token distribution mechanism through its Curator Program.

Curators stake GRT tokens to signal which subgraphs (indexed data) they believe are the most useful. This
mechanism aligns the interests of token holders with the quality of data provided by the protocol.

Future Trends in Token Creation and Distribution

Looking ahead, we can expect to see further innovation in token creation and distribution mechanisms. Here are a few trends to watch:

- **Fair Launches:** Inspired by the success of Bitcoin, which had no pre-mine or token sale, more projects may opt for "fair launches" where tokens are distributed to users through mining or other participatory activities.

- **Community Governance:** More projects may distribute tokens to their users to enable community governance. This aligns with the ethos of decentralization, as it gives users a say in the project's development.

- **Regulated Token Sales:** As regulatory clarity improves, we may see more projects conducting regulated token sales, offering investors more security and legal protections.

- **Cross-Chain Interoperability:** With the rise of cross-chain interoperability, tokens may be distributed across multiple blockchains, broadening their reach and utility.

In conclusion, the future of token creation and distribution looks bright, with many exciting developments on the horizon. As we continue to explore and innovate in this space, we can expect to see more efficient, fair, and inclusive token economies emerging.

9.7: The Future of Token Valuation

Understanding the Current State of Token Valuation Models

Token valuation models are currently in a nascent stage, with many different models being experimented with.

Some of the most common models include the utility token valuation model, where the value of a token is derived from its utility within a specific ecosystem, and the security token valuation model, which is similar to traditional equity valuation models.

However, these models have their limitations. For instance, utility token valuation models often struggle to accurately capture the value of a token due to the volatile nature of the token's utility.

Similarly, security token valuation models may not always be applicable, as not all tokens represent ownership of an underlying asset.

How Emerging Trends are Shaping the Future of Token Valuation

As the blockchain industry continues to evolve, so too do the trends that are shaping the future of token valuation. One significant trend is the increasing importance of governance tokens, which give holders the right to vote on decisions within a particular ecosystem.

These tokens are often valued based on the perceived influence of the governance rights they provide, which can be difficult to quantify.

Another emerging trend is the rise of yield farming and liquidity mining, where tokens are distributed as rewards for providing liquidity to a protocol. This has led to the development of new valuation models that take into account the yield generated by these tokens.

Case Studies: Innovative Token Valuation Models

Let's look at two innovative token valuation models that have emerged recently:

Uniswap's UNI token: Uniswap, a decentralized exchange, introduced its UNI token as a governance token. The value of UNI is largely derived from the fees generated by the Uniswap protocol, which are distributed to UNI holders.

This has led to the development of a new valuation model that takes into account the expected future cash flows from these fees.

Yearn.finance's YFI token: Yearn.finance, a yield aggregator, introduced its YFI token as a governance token. Unlike UNI, YFI does not entitle holders to a share of the fees generated by the protocol. Instead, the value of YFI is derived from the perceived influence of the governance rights it provides.

This has led to the development of a new valuation model that attempts to quantify the value of these governance rights.

Future Trends in Token Valuation

Looking ahead, we can expect to see further innovation in token valuation models as new types of tokens and token functionalities emerge.

For instance, as more protocols adopt a DAO (Decentralized Autonomous Organization) structure, we may see the development of new valuation models that take into account the value of the governance rights provided by these DAOs.

Furthermore, as the DeFi sector continues to grow, we can expect to see more sophisticated valuation models that take into account the yield generated by DeFi tokens.

In conclusion, while token valuation is a complex and rapidly evolving field, it is clear that it will continue to play a crucial role in the future of Tokenomics.

As such, staying updated with the latest trends and developments in token valuation is essential for anyone interested in the blockchain and cryptocurrency space.

"In the ever-evolving landscape of cryptocurrency, preparation is key; it's like planting seeds today for a forest of opportunity tomorrow."
- Dennis Frank

9.8: The Future of Token Utility and Functionality

Understanding the Current State of Token Utility and Functionality

In the current state, tokens serve a multitude of purposes within the blockchain ecosystem. They are not just a medium of exchange or a store of value, but they also represent a wide range of digital assets and rights.

Tokens can represent anything from a real-world asset like real estate to digital services like cloud storage. They also play a crucial role in governance, decision-making, and incentivization within decentralized networks.

Emerging Trends Shaping the Future of Token Utility and Functionality

As the blockchain ecosystem evolves, we are witnessing several emerging trends that are shaping the future of token utility and functionality:

1. **Interoperability:** Interoperability is becoming increasingly important in the blockchain ecosystem. It allows different blockchain networks to interact and communicate with each other, thereby enhancing the utility and functionality of tokens. With interoperability, a token issued on one blockchain can potentially be used on another blockchain.

2. **Fractional Ownership:** Fractional ownership, facilitated by tokens, is another emerging trend. It allows multiple individuals to own a fraction of a high-value asset like real estate or artwork. This trend is likely to increase the utility of tokens, making them accessible to a wider audience.

3.   **Programmability:** With the advent of smart contracts, tokens have become programmable. This means that they can be programmed to perform specific functions or execute certain actions when predefined conditions are met. This adds a new dimension to the utility and functionality of tokens.

Case Studies: Innovative Uses of Token Utility and Functionality

1. Uniswap (UNI): Uniswap, a decentralized exchange, introduced its governance token, UNI, to allow users to participate in decision-making processes. UNI holders can vote on proposals and influence the future development of the platform. This is an innovative use of token utility, where tokens are used to decentralize governance and democratize decision-making.

2. Decentraland (MANA): Decentraland is a virtual reality platform where users can create, experience, and monetize content and applications. The platform's native token, MANA, is used to purchase virtual land and other digital goods within the Decentraland ecosystem.

This is an example of how tokens can be used to represent digital assets and facilitate transactions in a virtual economy.

Future Trends in Token Utility and Functionality

Looking ahead, we can expect the utility and functionality of tokens to continue to evolve and expand. Here are some potential future trends:

1. Tokenization of Everything: As blockchain technology matures, we could see the tokenization of a wide range of assets and rights, from intellectual property rights to carbon credits. This would significantly expand the utility and functionality of tokens.

2. Integration with IoT: With the integration of blockchain and Internet of Things (IoT), tokens could be used to facilitate machine-to-machine transactions in an IoT network.

3. Advanced Governance Models: As decentralized organizations become more prevalent, we could see more advanced governance models being implemented, with tokens playing a crucial role.

In conclusion, the future of token utility and functionality looks promising, with numerous innovations and advancements on the horizon.

As we continue to explore and understand the potential of blockchain technology, the role of tokens in this ecosystem is likely to become even more significant and diverse.

"The stock market is filled with individuals who know the price of everything, but the value of nothing." - Philip Fisher

9.9: Emerging Trends and Future of Tokenomics: A Recap

Welcome to the final lesson of our comprehensive course on mastering Tokenomics. We have covered a lot of ground, from understanding the basic concepts of Tokenomics to exploring its various aspects such as types of digital tokens, token creation and distribution mechanisms, economic models, regulatory landscape, case studies, market dynamics, utility and functionality of tokens, and emerging trends.

In this final lesson, we will recap the emerging trends in Tokenomics and discuss the future of this fascinating field.

Recap of the Emerging Trends in Tokenomics

Throughout this course, we have touched upon several emerging trends in Tokenomics. Let's revisit some of the key developments:

1. **Decentralized Finance (DeFi) and Yield Farming**: DeFi has emerged as a revolutionary trend in the blockchain space, with tokens playing a crucial role in these decentralized applications. Yield farming, where users earn tokens as a reward for providing liquidity, has become a popular trend in DeFi.

2. **Rise of DAOs and Community Governance**: Decentralized Autonomous Organizations (DAOs) are entities that are run by smart contracts on a blockchain. The rise of DAOs has led to a new trend of community governance, where token holders have a say in the decision-making process.

3. **Intersection of Tokenomics and Traditional Finance**: As blockchain technology matures, we are seeing an increasing intersection of Tokenomics and traditional finance. This is leading to the creation of new financial products and services that leverage the benefits of both worlds.

Future of Tokenomics

The future of Tokenomics is promising and full of potential. As blockchain technology continues to evolve, we can expect to see new types of tokens and innovative token models.

Regulatory frameworks around the world will also continue to evolve to accommodate these developments. The rise of DeFi and DAOs suggests that tokens will play an increasingly important role in the decentralized economy.

Staying Updated with the Latest Trends in Tokenomics

The field of Tokenomics is dynamic and rapidly evolving. To stay updated with the latest trends, it is recommended to follow reputable blockchain news sources, participate in blockchain communities, and attend industry events and webinars.

Regularly reading research papers and articles on Tokenomics can also help deepen your understanding and keep you abreast of the latest developments.

Final Thoughts on the Future of Tokenomics

As we conclude this course, it is clear that Tokenomics is not just a theoretical concept but a practical framework that is shaping the future of digital economies. With the rise of blockchain technology, digital tokens have become an integral part of our digital lives.

As Tokenomics continues to evolve, it will play a crucial role in shaping the future of decentralized systems, impacting everything from finance and governance to digital ownership and beyond.

Thank you for joining us on this journey to master Tokenomics. We hope that this course has provided you with a solid foundation and sparked your curiosity to continue exploring this fascinating field. Happy learning!

"Tokenomics: the heartbeat of blockchain projects, where each token beats to its own rhythm, shaping success, functionality, and the balance of risk and reward." - - - Dennis Frank

Glossary of Tokenomics Terms

Airdrops: A distribution of free tokens to a group of cryptocurrency holders.

Altcoins: Alternative cryptocurrencies other than Bitcoin, such as Ethereum, Litecoin, or Ripple.

Anti-Money Laundering (AML) Compliance: Regulations and procedures designed to prevent the illegal use of cryptocurrencies for money laundering.

Artificial Intelligence (AI) in Token Distribution: The use of AI technology to optimize the distribution of tokens in a cryptocurrency project.

Basic Attention Token (BAT): A cryptocurrency used in the Brave browser ecosystem to reward users for their attention to ads and content.

Bearish and Bullish Sentiment: Market sentiment indicating pessimism (bearish) or optimism (bullish) about the future price of a cryptocurrency.

Binance Coin (BNB) Utility: The utility and functions of Binance Coin within the Binance cryptocurrency exchange platform.

Bitcoin (BTC): The first and most well-known cryptocurrency, often referred to as digital gold.

Bitcoin (BTC) Token Model: The structure and properties of Bitcoin as a token, including its supply and use cases.

Bitcoin Bull Run: A period of rapid and sustained price increase in the Bitcoin market.

Bitcoin Halving: An event that occurs approximately every four years, reducing the rate at which new Bitcoin is created, halving the block reward.

BitConnect Ponzi Scheme: A fraudulent cryptocurrency scheme that promised high returns but collapsed as a Ponzi scheme.

Blockchain: A distributed ledger technology used to record and verify transactions in a secure and transparent manner.

Blockchain Capital (BCAP): A cryptocurrency token representing ownership in a blockchain-focused venture capital fund.

Blockchain Ecosystem: The interconnected network of blockchain projects, technologies, and participants.

Blockchain Project Ambitions and Regulations: The goals and regulatory compliance considerations of blockchain-based projects.

Blockchain Protocol: The set of rules and standards governing how blockchain networks operate and communicate.

Blockchain Scalability Solutions: Technologies and techniques to increase the transaction processing capacity of blockchain networks.

Blockchain Security Measures: Measures and techniques implemented to secure blockchain networks and data.

Blockchain Technology: The underlying technology that powers cryptocurrencies and decentralized applications.

Blockchain Technology Legal Aspects: Legal considerations and regulations related to the use and adoption of blockchain technology.

Blockchain-based Gaming Economies: The use of blockchain technology to create in-game economies and assets.

Burn-and-Mint Equilibrium Model: A tokenomics model where tokens are burned (destroyed) and minted (created) to maintain balance.

Burniske's Equation of Exchange: A formula used to estimate the network value of cryptocurrencies.

Central Bank Digital Currencies (CBDCs): Digital currencies issued and regulated by central banks.

China's Crypto Ban: The restrictions and prohibitions imposed by the Chinese government on cryptocurrency activities.

China's ICO Ban: The ban on Initial Coin Offerings (ICOs) in China due to regulatory concerns.

Commodity Futures Trading Commission (CFTC): A U.S. regulatory agency responsible for overseeing commodity futures and options markets.

Comparables Analysis in Tokenomics: A financial analysis method that compares a token's valuation to similar tokens or assets.

Compliance Costs in Tokenomics: The expenses associated with meeting regulatory compliance requirements in token projects.

Compliance Requirements: The rules and regulations that token projects must adhere to, often related to anti-money laundering (AML), and know your customer (KYC) regulations.

Consumer Protection Laws in Tokenomics: Regulations designed to protect cryptocurrency users and investors from fraudulent practices.

Contractual Risks in Token Management: Risks associated with the legal contracts and agreements governing token issuance and management.

Cost of Production Model: A tokenomics model that calculates a token's value based on its production and maintenance costs.

Counter-Terrorism Financing (CTF) Laws: Legal measures aimed at preventing the use of cryptocurrencies for financing terrorism.

Cross-Chain Transactions: Transactions involving the transfer of assets or data between different blockchain networks.

Cryptocurrency: Digital or virtual currencies that use cryptography for security and operate independently of a central authority.

Cryptocurrency Exchanges: Platforms that facilitate the buying, selling, and trading of cryptocurrencies.

Cryptocurrency Market Volatility: The degree of price fluctuation in cryptocurrency markets.

Cryptocurrency Regulatory Environment: The regulatory framework and policies governing the use and trading of cryptocurrencies.

Cryptocurrency Speculative Nature: The tendency of cryptocurrencies to be driven by speculation rather than intrinsic value.

Customer Due Diligence (CDD): The process of verifying and identifying cryptocurrency customers as part of anti-money laundering (AML) regulations.

Customer Identification Program (CIP): Procedures and protocols for verifying the identity of cryptocurrency customers.

DAO Case Study: An examination of the Decentralized Autonomous Organization (DAO) incident, a significant event in cryptocurrency history.

DAOs (Decentralized Autonomous Organizations): Smart contract-driven organizations that operate autonomously on the blockchain.

Data Analytics in Token Valuation: The use of data analysis techniques to assess the value of cryptocurrency tokens.

Decentralized Autonomous Organization (DAO): An organization governed by smart contracts and run by its members on the blockchain.

Decentralized Autonomous Organizations (DAOs): Multiple decentralized autonomous organizations operating within the blockchain space.

Decentralized Finance (DeFi): A movement in the cryptocurrency space that aims to create decentralized financial systems and services.

Decentralized Finance (DeFi) Impact: The influence of DeFi on traditional financial systems and services.

Decentralized Venture Capital Funds: Venture capital funds that operate in a decentralized manner on blockchain networks.

Delegated Proof-of-Stake (DPoS): A consensus algorithm used in blockchain networks where participants vote for representatives to validate transactions.

Deflationary Models in Tokenomics: Tokenomics models in which the token supply decreases over time.

Deflationary Token Models: Tokens with a decreasing supply, designed to increase in value over time.

Digital Economies: Economic systems that rely on digital assets, including cryptocurrencies and digital tokens.

Digital Token Ecosystem Integrity: Ensuring the trustworthiness and reliability of digital token ecosystems.

Digital Tokens: Cryptographic assets or tokens issued on blockchain networks.

Digital Tokens Regulations: Regulatory guidelines and rules governing the issuance and use of digital tokens.

Discounted Cash Flow (DCF) Model: A financial model used to estimate the present value of future cash flows associated with a token.

Eater Address in Tokenomics: A specific address on the Ethereum blockchain where tokens are irrecoverably sent, effectively removing them from circulation.

Economic Models in Tokenomics: The models and theories used to understand the economic dynamics of cryptocurrencies and tokens.

Elon Musk's Market Influence: The impact of Elon Musk's tweets and statements on cryptocurrency markets.

Enhanced Due Diligence (EDD): A more comprehensive and in-depth process for verifying customer identities and assessing risk in the cryptocurrency space.

Environmental Impact of Blockchain: The assessment of blockchain technology's ecological footprint and its energy consumption.

Equity Tokens: Tokens that represent ownership or equity in a company or project.

ERC-20: A widely adopted token standard on the Ethereum blockchain that defines a set of rules and functions for creating tokens.

ERC-20 Token Standard: The standard protocol for creating fungible tokens on the Ethereum blockchain.

ERC-721: A token standard on the Ethereum blockchain for creating non-fungible tokens (NFTs), each with a unique identity.

Ether (ETH) and Network Effects: The impact of Ethereum's native cryptocurrency, Ether, on the growth and adoption of the Ethereum network.

Ethereum: A blockchain platform that enables the creation of decentralized applications (DApps) and smart contracts.

Ethereum (ETH) and Smart Contracts: The role of Ether (ETH) in facilitating smart contracts on the Ethereum blockchain.

Ethereum Classic: A fork of the Ethereum blockchain that maintains the original Ethereum blockchain after a contentious hard fork.

Ethereum's Economic Model: The economic principles and incentives that govern the Ethereum network.

Ethereum's PoW to PoS Transition: Ethereum's transition from a Proof-of-Work (PoW) consensus mechanism to a Proof-of-Stake (PoS) mechanism.

Ethereum's SEC Ruling: Regulatory decisions and actions related to Ethereum by the U.S. Securities and Exchange Commission (SEC).

European Securities and Markets Authority (ESMA): A European Union regulatory agency overseeing securities and financial markets.

Fair Launch: A token distribution method where tokens are distributed fairly and without pre-sale advantages.

Fair Launch Model: A token distribution model that prioritizes fairness and equal access to tokens.

Filecoin (FIL): A cryptocurrency and decentralized storage network designed to facilitate data storage and retrieval.

Financial Crimes Enforcement Network (FinCEN): A U.S. regulatory agency responsible for combating financial crimes, including money laundering.

Financial Services Agency (FSA): The Japanese regulatory authority overseeing financial markets and institutions.

Forks: Divisions or splits in a blockchain network that create separate chains with different rules.

Fractional Ownership: The ownership of a fraction or share of an asset, often facilitated by blockchain tokens.

Fungible Tokens: Tokens that are interchangeable with each other and have identical values.

Future Trends in Token Valuation: Predictions and expectations regarding the valuation of tokens in the future.

Global Regulatory Frameworks: The various regulatory approaches and frameworks applied to cryptocurrencies and tokens worldwide.

Governance in DeFi Tokens: The mechanisms and processes for decentralized decision-making in decentralized finance (DeFi) projects.

Governance Tokens: Tokens that grant holders the ability to participate in the governance and decision-making of a blockchain project or platform.

Hybrid Models: Tokenomics models that combine elements of different models, such as inflationary and deflationary features.

Hybrid Models in Tokenomics: Tokenomics models that incorporate a blend of different economic principles.

ICO Regulation Impact: The effects of regulatory actions and changes on Initial Coin Offerings (ICOs).

Immutability: The quality of blockchain records and transactions being irreversible and unchangeable once confirmed.

Incentive Structures in Tokenomics: The rewards and incentives designed to encourage desired behaviors within a token ecosystem.

Incentivized Holding: Encouraging token holders to retain and not sell their tokens through incentives.

Inflationary Models in Tokenomics: Tokenomics models in which the token supply increases over time.

Initial Coin Offerings (ICOs): Fundraising events where new tokens or cryptocurrencies are sold to investors.

Initial Coin Offerings (ICOs) Ban: The prohibition or restriction of ICOs in various jurisdictions.

Institutional Participation: Involvement of traditional financial institutions and large organizations in the cryptocurrency space.

Interoperability: The ability of different blockchain networks to communicate and interact with each other.

Interoperability in Tokenomics: The consideration of how tokens can function across multiple blockchain platforms.

Investor Protection: Measures and regulations aimed at safeguarding the interests of cryptocurrency investors.

Investor Protection in Tokenomics: Efforts to ensure that investors are informed, secure, and protected when participating in token projects.

Investor Sentiment: The collective feelings and beliefs of cryptocurrency investors, which can influence market behavior.

Jurisdictional Differences in Token Regulation: Variances in cryptocurrency regulations and rules across different regions and jurisdictions.

Know Your Customer (KYC) Compliance: Verification processes for identifying and confirming the identity of cryptocurrency customers.

Know Your Customer in Blockchain: The application of KYC principles within blockchain-based systems.

Legal Accountability in DAOs: Determining legal responsibility and liability in the context of Decentralized Autonomous Organizations (DAOs).

Legal and Regulatory Compliance: Adherence to laws and regulations governing cryptocurrencies and token projects.

Legal and Regulatory Considerations: Factors related to the legal and regulatory environment that impact token projects.

Legal Aspects of Anti-Money Laundering: The legal framework and requirements for combating money laundering in the cryptocurrency industry.

Legal Framework: The set of laws and regulations governing the use and operation of cryptocurrencies and tokens.

Legal Framework in Tokenomics: The legal structure that surrounds the issuance and management of tokens.

Legal Risk Management in Token Issuance: Strategies for mitigating legal risks associated with token issuance.

Libra/Diem Project Case Study: An examination of Facebook's Libra/Diem cryptocurrency project.

Liquidity Mining: The process of earning rewards by providing liquidity to decentralized exchanges and liquidity pools.

Liquidity Mining in DeFi: The use of liquidity mining programs in decentralized finance (DeFi) protocols.

Liquidity Tokens: Tokens that facilitate liquidity provision in decentralized exchanges and DeFi platforms.

Litigation Risks in Tokenomics: Legal risks and potential disputes that can arise in token projects.

Machine Learning in Crypto Valuation: The use of machine learning techniques to assess and predict cryptocurrency valuations.

Machine Learning in Token Distribution: The application of machine learning algorithms to optimize token distribution strategies.

Macroeconomic Factors in Crypto: The impact of broader economic trends and events on the cryptocurrency market.

Markets in Crypto-Assets (MiCA) Regulation: European Union regulatory framework aimed at regulating crypto-assets and related services.

Market Dynamics: The forces and factors that influence price movements and behavior in cryptocurrency markets.

Market Dynamics in Tokenomics: Understanding how market forces affect the value and behavior of tokens.

Market Manipulation in Crypto: Illicit activities aimed at artificially influencing cryptocurrency prices.

Market Sentiment: The overall sentiment and mood of cryptocurrency market participants.

Market Sentiment in Tokenomics: The influence of market sentiment on token prices and behavior.

Market Volatility: The degree of price fluctuation in cryptocurrency markets.

Medium of Exchange: The function of cryptocurrencies as a means of conducting transactions and payments.

Metcalfe's Law in Crypto: A principle suggesting that the value of a network is proportional to the square of the number of its users.

Mining: The process of validating transactions and adding them to a blockchain, often requiring significant computational power.

Monetary Sovereignty and Digital Currencies: The concept of control over a nation's currency and the implications of digital currencies.

Net Asset Value (NAV) Model: A token valuation model that calculates a token's value based on its underlying assets.

Network Effects in Tokenomics: The positive impact of a growing user base on the value and adoption of a token.

Network Participants: Individuals or entities that participate in a blockchain or cryptocurrency network, such as users, miners, validators, and nodes.

Network Value to Transactions (NVT) Ratio: A metric used to evaluate the valuation of a cryptocurrency by comparing its market capitalization to its transaction volume.

News Influence on Crypto Market: The impact of news, events, and public sentiment on the prices and behaviors of cryptocurrencies.

Non-Fungible Tokens (NFTs): Unique digital assets representing ownership or proof of authenticity of a specific item or piece of content, often used in art, collectibles, and gaming.

Ongoing Monitoring in Token Management: Continuous supervision and tracking of tokens to ensure their proper functionality and security.

Participation Model in Tokenomics: A framework that outlines how individuals or entities can participate in the governance and operation of a blockchain network.

Payment Tokens: Cryptocurrencies or tokens primarily designed for facilitating transactions and payments.

Ponzi Scheme: A fraudulent investment scheme that promises high returns to earlier investors, paid with the capital of newer investors, rather than from legitimate profits.

Price Stability in Tokenomics: Maintaining a stable value for a cryptocurrency or token to reduce volatility and encourage its use as a medium of exchange.

Price Trends Analysis: The examination of historical price data to identify patterns and predict future price movements.

Programmability: The ability to execute code or scripts on a blockchain, commonly associated with smart contracts.

Proof of Stake (PoS): A consensus mechanism in blockchain networks where validators are chosen to create new blocks and confirm transactions based on the amount of cryptocurrency they hold and are willing to "stake" as collateral.

Proof of Work (PoW): A consensus mechanism where miners compete to solve complex mathematical puzzles to create new blocks and secure the blockchain network.

Quantity Theory of Money in Tokenomics: A theory that explores the relationship between the money supply, the velocity of money, and the overall price level in an economy.

Real Estate Tokenization: The process of converting physical real estate assets into digital tokens on a blockchain, making it easier to buy and sell fractional ownership.

Regulatory Bodies: Government or independent agencies responsible for overseeing and enforcing regulations related to cryptocurrencies and blockchain technology.

Regulatory Challenges in Tokenomics: Obstacles and issues related to complying with regulatory requirements in the tokenomics space.

Regulatory Compliance: Adhering to legal and regulatory requirements imposed by authorities governing the use and issuance of tokens.

Regulatory Compliance in Cryptocurrencies: Ensuring that cryptocurrency activities and transactions comply with relevant laws and regulations.

Regulatory Compliance in Tokenomics: Compliance with regulations specific to the design and management of tokens and token-based systems.

Regulatory Impact on Token Pricing: The influence of government regulations on the value and trading of tokens.

Regulatory Landscape: The overall framework of regulations and laws that affect the cryptocurrency and tokenomics industry.

Regulatory News: Updates and announcements from regulatory authorities regarding their stance on cryptocurrencies and tokens.

Regulatory Scrutiny in Tokenomics: Intense examination and investigation by regulatory bodies into token-related activities.

Regulatory Uncertainty in Digital Tokens: Lack of clarity and predictability regarding future regulations in the digital token space.

Risk Assessment in Tokenomics: The process of evaluating potential risks and vulnerabilities in token-based projects.

Risk Management in Tokenomics: Strategies and actions taken to mitigate and manage risks associated with token-based systems.

Scarcity in Tokenomics: The concept of limiting the supply of tokens to create scarcity and potentially increase their value.

Securities and Exchange Commission (SEC): A U.S. regulatory agency responsible for enforcing securities laws and regulating financial markets.

Securities Laws Compliance: Compliance with laws that govern the issuance and trading of securities, which can apply to certain tokens.

Security in Token Projects: Measures and practices implemented to protect token-based systems from security threats and vulnerabilities.

Security Token Offering (STO): A fundraising method where tokens are issued that represent ownership in an asset or company and comply with securities regulations.

Security Tokens: Tokens that represent ownership of a real-world asset, company equity, or other financial instruments, subject to securities regulations.

Smart Contract: Self-executing contracts with the terms of the agreement directly written into code, often used on blockchain platforms.

Smart Contract Vulnerabilities: Weaknesses or flaws in the code of a smart contract that can be exploited by malicious actors.

Social Media Sentiment Analysis: Analyzing social media posts and discussions to gauge public sentiment and its potential impact on cryptocurrency markets.

Stability Tokens: Cryptocurrencies designed to maintain a stable value, often pegged to a traditional fiat currency or asset.

Staking: Participating in a proof-of-stake blockchain network by locking up cryptocurrency as collateral to support network operations.

Staking Model in Tokenomics: A system that outlines how stakers are rewarded for their participation in a proof-of-stake blockchain.

Stock Exchange Commission (SEC): A regulatory body responsible for overseeing and regulating stock exchanges and securities markets.

Store of Value: An asset that can be reliably saved, retrieved, and exchanged over time, retaining its value.

Success and Failure in Token Projects: Assessing the outcomes of token-based projects based on their objectives and performance.

Supply and Demand in Tokenomics: The interaction between the availability of tokens and the desire to obtain them, affecting their price.

Supply Chain Management via Blockchain: Using blockchain technology to track and verify the movement and authenticity of products in supply chains.

Supply Management in Tokenomics: Strategies and mechanisms for controlling the issuance and distribution of tokens.

Tezos ICO Challenges: Challenges and controversies surrounding the initial coin offering (ICO) of the Tezos blockchain project.

The DAO Case Study: An infamous case where a decentralized autonomous organization (DAO) was exploited, resulting in a contentious hard fork in the Ethereum blockchain.

The Howey Test: A legal test used to determine whether an investment qualifies as a security under U.S. securities laws.

Token Burn Mechanisms: A process of deliberately destroying or removing a certain quantity of tokens from circulation.

Token Concentration: The distribution of tokens among a small number of holders, potentially impacting market dynamics.

Token Creation: The process of generating new tokens, often through mining or minting.

Token Demand: The desire and willingness of individuals or entities to acquire and hold tokens.

Token Distribution: The process of distributing tokens to initial investors, users, or stakeholders

Token Distribution Mechanisms: Methods used to allocate tokens to various participants in a fair and equitable manner.

Token Economies: Systems where tokens are used as a medium of exchange within a specific ecosystem or community.

Token Functionality: The specific features and capabilities of a token within a blockchain ecosystem.

Token Interoperability: The ability of tokens to function across different blockchain platforms and networks.

Token Issuance Legal Challenges: Legal issues and compliance requirements associated with creating and issuing tokens.

Token Models: Various models and designs for tokens, such as utility tokens, security tokens, and stablecoins.

Token Price vs. Token Value: Distinguishing between the market price of a token and its inherent value or utility.

Token Pricing Factors: Factors that influence the market price of a token, including supply, demand, and external events.

Token Project Analysis: Evaluating the viability, goals, and execution of a token-based project.

Token Sale: An event where tokens are offered to the public, often as part of an initial coin offering (ICO) or security token offering (STO).

Token Scarcity and Value: The relationship between limited token supply and potential increases in value.

Token Standards: Protocols and standards that define the rules and behaviors of tokens on a blockchain.

Token Supply: The total quantity of tokens created and available within a blockchain ecosystem.

Token Trading Volume Analysis: Examining the volume of token trades on exchanges to gain insights into market activity.

Token Utility: The usefulness and functionality of a token within a specific ecosystem or network.

Token Valuation: Assessing the worth or value of a token based on various factors.

Token Valuation Models: Mathematical and economic models used to estimate the value of tokens.

Token Velocity: The rate at which tokens change hands within a blockchain ecosystem.

Token-Based Governance: Systems where token holders have a say in the decision-making and governance of a blockchain project.

Tokenization: The process of converting real-world assets, such as real estate or stocks, into digital tokens on a blockchain.

Tokenization of Assets: Using blockchain technology to represent ownership or rights to physical or digital assets as tokens.

Tokenomics: The study of the economic and financial principles governing the design and use of tokens.

Tokens: Digital or cryptographic assets that represent value and can be used for various purposes within blockchain ecosystems.

Traditional Finance: Conventional financial systems and institutions outside the realm of cryptocurrencies and blockchain

Traditional Finance in Crypto Valuation: Incorporating traditional financial methods and metrics to assess the value of cryptocurrencies.

Transaction Costs in Tokenomics: Fees associated with executing transactions on a blockchain network.

Transparency: The degree to which information and data within a blockchain ecosystem are openly accessible and verifiable.

Unit of Account: A standard measure or unit used to value and express prices within an economic system.

User Behavior Incentivization: Encouraging specific behaviors or actions by rewarding users with tokens or other incentives.

User Experience in Blockchain: The overall satisfaction and usability of blockchain applications and platforms for users.

Utility Tokens: Tokens that provide access to specific products or services within a blockchain ecosystem.

Value Creation in Tokenomics: The generation of value within a token-based system through various mechanisms.

Value Transfer in Tokenomics: The process of transferring value from one participant to another within a blockchain network.

Web 3.0: An evolving concept of the internet that envisions a decentralized, user-centric, and blockchain-powered web.

Whitepaper: A document that outlines the goals, technology, and structure of a blockchain project or cryptocurrency.

Wrapped Tokens: Tokens that represent other assets, such as cryptocurrencies or assets from other blockchains.

Yield Farming: A DeFi (Decentralized Finance) practice where users provide liquidity to earn rewards or interest on their holdings.

Yield Farming in Tokenomics: Incorporating yield farming strategies to incentivize participation and liquidity in token-based systems.

Zero-Knowledge Proofs: Cryptographic techniques that allow one party to prove knowledge of a fact without revealing the specific details, ensuring privacy and security.

Meet the Course Creator

Dennis Frank, a seasoned veteran of the mining industry, transitioned from a 43-year career to pursue his passion for the digital world, focusing on website development and content creation in the realms of AI, cryptocurrency and blockchain. Dennis's journey is a testament to his belief in continuous learning and adaptation.

Originally a music major at the University of Northern Colorado (UNC), Dennis's love for the arts seamlessly blends with his technical acumen. His curiosity and dedication to understanding the intricacies of AI, blockchain, and cryptocurrency, have given him a voice in the digital community.

From the Mines to the Digital World

Dennis's transition from mining to digital content creation symbolizes a bridge between traditional industries and the burgeoning world of technology. His approach to explaining complex concepts in these subjects is deeply rooted in his own journey of discovery and education, making his content relatable and easy to understand.

Published Works

1. **Mastering Tokenomics: The Ultimate Guide** – A comprehensive exploration of digital tokens and their impact on the economy, ideated and compiled by Dennis to simplify the world of blockchain for enthusiasts and professionals alike.

2. **AI Unveiled: Navigating the Intersection of Technology, Ethics, and Society** - This book demystifies AI, breaking it down into understandable components, emphasizing that AI is not just about replicating human intelligence but about creating tools to assist in daily tasks, problem-solving, and fostering discoveries beyond our current capabilities.

3. **Crypto Currency Investment Strategies: A Comprehensive Guide** - This book is an essential resource for beginners, offering a deep dive into the intricacies of cryptocurrency investment.

4. **Blockchain Unlocked: Navigating the Digital Ledger Revolution** - This book demystifies the complex world of blockchain, offering readers a clear understanding of what it is, how it works, and why it's rapidly becoming one of the most significant technological advancements of our time.

5. **The Moral Ledger: The Believers Guide to Cryptocurrency Investment.** An essential primer at the intersection of Christian values and the rapidly changing world of digital finance and integrating faith with financial decisions

6. **The Digital Chronicles: Ai Through a Theological Lens: A** comprehensive exploration of the increasingly influential world of Artificial Intelligence through the lens of Christian theology.

Life Beyond Writing

When not immersed in the digital world, Dennis is an avid fisherman and camper, finding solace in the serene landscapes of northeast Wyoming. A guitar enthusiast, he enjoys playing and teaching music, sharing the joy of melodies just as he shares knowledge in technology.

Married to Eva for 47 years, and a proud father to David and Christina, Dennis values family above all. His involvement in praise and worship at his local church showcases his commitment to community and faith.

Connect with Dennis Frank

Stay in tune with Dennis's latest explorations in blockchain and cryptocurrency by visiting his website.

Discover engaging articles, informative videos, and insightful podcasts, all designed to enlighten and educate.

- Website: KryptoKraken.com
- Author Profile: www.amazon.com/author/Dennis-Frank

A Note from Dennis

"I've always believed that the best way to understand a subject is to teach it. Sharing my journey into the world of blockchain and cryptocurrency has been an enriching experience, and I hope my work helps demystify this fascinating field for others.

Thank you for joining me on this journey of continuous learning and discovery. Here's to exploring new horizons and living life to its fullest!"
-Dennis Frank

Support my Work: paypal.me/kryptokraken

"Tokenomics: A journey beyond currencies, crafting the DNA of tomorrow's decentralized world." -Dennis Frank